7 c '/10

A Guitar
and a Pen

★ ★ ★

A Guitar
and a Pen

★ ★ ★

STORIES BY COUNTRY MUSIC'S
GREATEST SONGWRITERS

Edited by

ROBERT HICKS

Coedited by John Bohlinger and Justin Stelter

CENTER
STREET

New York Boston Nashville

Center Street
Hachette Book Group USA
237 Park Avenue
New York, NY 10017

Visit our Web site at www.centerstreet.com

Center Street is a division of Hachette Book Group USA, Inc.
The Center Street name and logo are trademarks of
Hachette Book Group USA, Inc.

Printed in the United States of America

First edition: May 2008

10   9   8   7   6   5   4   3   2   1

Library of Congress Cataloging-in-Publication Data

A guitar and a pen : stories by country music's greatest songwriters / edited by Robert Hicks ; coedited by John Bohlinger and Justin Stelter. — 1st ed.
p. cm.
Summary: "Robert Hicks presents a collection of stories written by country music's greatest songwriters"— Provided by the publisher.
ISBN-13: 978-1-59995-064-8
ISBN-10: 1-59995-064-2
1. Short stories, American.   2. American fiction—
21st century.   I. Hicks, Robert, 1951–   II. Bohlinger, John.
III. Stelter, Justin.   IV. Title.

PS648.S5G85 2008
813'.010806—dc22
2007043672

Contents

CONTENTS

Foreword

Vince Gill

Like so many folks my age, I grew up on story songs. Those unforgettable tales always cut me to the quick, whether they were heartbreaking or sidesplitting. I carried them with me, humming their melodies while I lived my young years through their stories. They taught me a thing or two about what life was like before mine had even really begun. They're a real part of what first drew me to country music. I guess I'm not alone in that way. And as they're at the core of why so many of us were first drawn to the music, they remain at the core—at the heart—of why we've never forsaken our first love for it.

When I finally came to Nashville, I had the privilege to meet and, in time, befriend some of the finest songwriters ever to put words to paper. I count it as one of the greatest honors and privileges ever bestowed on me, to live and work among them. Over the years, after countless songwriting sessions, you realize that some of the greatest songwriters around are also some of the best storytellers. You learn pretty quickly that a beautiful voice will never grab you as tightly if the words aren't right.

As one who's been plugging away at songwriting for a while

now, I know for sure when I'm in the company of the "greats." These songwriters know their craft back to front. They know how to pull a line out of the air that a young child and a grown man can both understand. In less than three minutes, they manage to create a lifetime of emotion. Now some of them have broken loose with these beautifully written short stories for all of us.

Just as Marty Robbins once told us in two minutes and fifty-eight seconds the epic tale of a cowboy who meets a beautiful girl, kills the rival for her hand in a gunfight, steals a horse, runs away, returns to the girl, takes a bullet, kisses the girl, and dies, these men and women are spinning their tales a little longer this time. If the story-songwriter is the ultimate short, short story writer, then what can he do when he has a bit more time and paper? That question remains at the center of this collection.

A Guitar and a Pen is a long-overdue celebration of the talent of not just these writers, but of all of country music's storytellers. Like songs, some of the stories are true, others are fiction, and a few are a bit of both. Looking through these pages, you'll find the work of many of the artists who made country music what it is. The history of great country songs goes back before any of us were around and will be here long after we're gone.

Just like a good country song, *A Guitar and a Pen* will prove to be the perfect companion for a long winter evening by a fire or a lazy summer afternoon in a hammock. So there you have it, right there in your hands, the words and stories of some of my all-time favorites. Dig in and enjoy!

A Guitar
and a Pen

★ ★ ★

The Day Jimmy
Killed the Rabbit

Tom T. Hall

On television we see that the cold-weather fronts from Canada sweep down into southern Missouri, turn left, and head back north. The day Jimmy killed the rabbit there were no TV sets in rural southern Missouri. At Jimmy's house, there was no electricity. The lone radio was powered by battery. The house where Jimmy and his father, mother, and two brothers lived was heated with wood-burning stoves.

It had rained on the crystallized snow. The rain had frozen, and now the countryside was covered with a crusty blanket of ice.

The old Ford automobile that sat in the front of the wood-framed house had long been inoperative. The battery had been removed from the old car to power the Zenith radio that brought the news of the New Deal era. Every afternoon Jimmy's father sat with his ear to the radio, listening for news of the Roosevelt administration's efforts to bring the country out of the Great Depression. Jimmy's father turned off the radio and turned to his family huddled around the stove in the small living room.

"They say he's gonna put poets and artists to work, too. Now there's a man who's got crazy on one shoulder and common sense on the other."

The mother made an almost inaudible comment. The children took it as bad news if the father thought so. The father continued. "What we need is jobs for the people. All this high talk about building parks and drawing pictures is crazy. They's folks starving to death."

Jimmy got up and left the room. He thought his father might have heard some good news and then let them listen to a good radio show, as he sometimes did.

There was a small barn and a separate chicken house behind the residence. The barn was long lonesome of cattle, and there were no chickens left. A late afternoon sun glanced across the sparkling ice and snow, hurting the eyes. Jimmy pulled the old door of the chicken house aside. He walked into the cold darkness of the building. In a far corner, surrounded by several old bales of hay, there stood a crudely crafted rabbit hutch. The top was covered with an old board. Jimmy lifted the board and reached inside the hutch and retrieved a little white rabbit. The animal kicked once with its powerful back legs; the boy struggled to hold it. The rabbit settled in the arms of the boy as he called it by name and stroked its downy fur. The rabbit had been an Easter present to a friend of Jimmy's. The friend could not feed the pet, and so Jimmy had brought it home. The boy was delighted to find that the rabbit would eat the bran cereal that came in plain white boxes from the relief agency that supplied the area families with food. A government official had decided that the rural people needed the bran because of the high fat content of their diets. After having choked on the cereal, Jimmy's father had banned it from the table. And so, the rabbit ate.

*   *   *

JIMMY'S UNCLE, on his father's side, lived a few hundred yards up the dirt road. The uncle was a dying man of sixty-seven years, a retired railroad man of considerable means, if one compared his worth to the average of the area, and that amounted to comparing his worth to poverty. There's hope in a dying uncle who has money, and such was the hope of Jimmy's family on these cold winter days of want and need. The family cared for the old bachelor uncle in a fashion that made the uncle suspicious of their motives. He would say, "When I was a well man, it seemed like you-all never paid me no mind at all. Now that I'm sick, it seems you-all are running up here with something or 'nother all the time. I've got my will made the way I want it made and ain't got no intention of changing it for a bowl of dried chicken soup and a two-day-old paper."

The contents of the mysterious will struck fear into the hearts of the family. Jimmy's mother had said more than once, "That old whoremonger probably got his will made out to some roundhouse hussie somewhere."

The father said, "I don't want none of my brother's money. I want a job and a chance to pull myself out of this hellhole we're into. He's lived a sinful life. His soul is of more concern than his stock."

Hope glimmers brightest in the darkest night. On a dark Sunday morning when the old battery that powered the radio gave up its last notion of life, Jimmy's mother returned from delivering hot food to the ailing uncle; she removed the heavy wool coat from her shoulders and announced, "I met Doc Witherspoon on the road. He says we ought to get your brother to a hospital if he's gonna live another day."

The father sat up on the sofa where he had been lying.

"How's he expect us to get him to a hospital? He won't go, anyway, and I can't carry him on my back."

"Well, you better get up there and sit with him then. I don't want none of the kids there when he dies. It'll give 'em nightmares."

The father cursed under his breath; he walked to the window and peered out at nothing. "I ain't no good with dying people either. I reckon he'd be just as well off alone. Lord knows he's managed to live alone. Don't see why he can't die alone."

"Don't you even think of that. That old man is your full blood brother and he's dying and you need to be there whether you like it or not."

"Don't shout at me, woman! I know who's my brother and who ain't. I've been around that man longer than most I reckon."

"Well, he's dying. It's on your shoulders. I've looked after him for more'n a year now. He ain't none of mine."

The children huddled in a corner of the room as the argument raged. The father picked up a coat from the floor and stormed out the door. The mother went to the window and watched her husband walk up the road toward the brother's house. "Reckon I was a little hard on him. But the truth's the truth, and it don't hurt to say it sometimes."

The youngest of the three boys spoke up. "How did Uncle hurt his heart?"

The mother turned and smiled at the child. "He hurt it by living too long and carrying on too much. Don't you think about it, honey. We're gonna be all right when your daddy finds work. Wait and see."

The father returned in less than an hour. He came quickly through the door and went directly to the kitchen. He spoke from there. "Ain't no coffee up there, and he's out of wood for the stove. Jimmy, get some wood and drag it down. I'll chop it. He wants a fried rabbit."

The mother went to the kitchen door. "He wants a fried rabbit?"

"That's what he said. He said his last request was a fried rabbit. I think he's getting out of his head a little. All he talked about was a fried rabbit."

"There ain't a rabbit in a hundred miles of this place. People have hunted down everything fit to eat."

The youngest boy spoke up. "Jimmy's got a rabbit."

All eyes turned to Jimmy. He was openmouthed. "It ain't no eatin' rabbit—it's a pettin' rabbit."

Jimmy stood and walked to the door. "I'll drag down some wood."

The youngest said, "A rabbit's a rabbit, if you ask me."

Jimmy turned at the door. "Well, nobody asked you, did they?"

Gray, low-hanging clouds surrounded the hilly countryside as Jimmy trudged up the hill behind his uncle's house. He carried an ax to cut free from the ice the fallen trees that he would bring down the hill for his father to chop into firewood. He spotted a limb he thought he could manage. He chopped away at the ice and snow that held it to the ground. Having grown up in the countryside, he knew instinctively what caught his eye as he swung the ax. It was a brown furry texture partially hidden by the snow and the limb. He swung the ax quickly. The furry creature kicked violently for a few seconds before settling into a motionless ball. Jimmy reached down and picked up the rabbit; he stared at the dead animal in awe. He turned and looked back down the hill as if he had been watched. Smoke rose from the chimney of his uncle's house. There was no one in sight.

The boy took his pocketknife from his trousers. He cut off

the rabbit's head. He slit the skin on the animal's back and pulled the warm fur from its back, legs, and neck. He cut off the feet and gutted the animal, throwing the intestines into the brush.

The boy walked into his uncle's house and held the rabbit aloft. The father stood from where he sat by the dying uncle. "Well, well, I'll be."

Jimmy continued to hold the rabbit aloft. The father came forward and took the rabbit from the boy. "Jimmy, that's a mighty big thing you done for your poor old uncle." He turned to the sick man and said, "Look what Jimmy's brought you. His own rabbit that he had for a pet. He wanted you to have what you wanted the most, and now he's brought you his own rabbit, much as he liked it."

Jimmy turned and walked out of the room and back to his wood-dragging chore. The old uncle leaned forward in his bed.

"That's a mighty fine boy, that Jimmy. Always said he was the best one of the bunch. Fine young man."

"I'll get the wife up here to cook this for you. She can make some biscuits and gravy to go with it."

"Fine, fine. Ain't had a meal like that since I don't know when. Don't know what's got into me. I've been hungry as a bear for some fried rabbit."

The old uncle and his brother sat talking as the mother fried the rabbit and made the biscuits and gravy. The father had fetched a jar of moonshine from the top of one of the cupboards. The house had a festive air. The brothers drank and seemingly became closer and more understanding as the jar of whiskey was passed back and forth. The mother cautioned against whiskey for the sick man. Her protests were laughed away.

The uncle became melancholy. He settled into a remorseful mood as the drinking continued. He began to apologize for his past sins. He hollered into the kitchen to tell his sister-in-law of his wrongdoings in life.

The afternoon's festivities ended with the uncle admitting that he had never had a will, but would now like to make one. He asked for pen and paper. He asked his brother to go up the road and bring down a neighbor to witness his last will and testament. With all of this done, the rabbit eaten, and the old wood-burning stove glowing, the uncle died at seven-fifteen that same evening.

As the undertaker drove past the house with the body of the old uncle, the father read the last will and testament of the man. The will left all of the uncle's earthly belongings to his nephew Jimmy. They would later learn that the inheritance included the house, thirty-six hundred dollars, and a gold railroad watch.

Jimmy stood in the middle of the room as the hero. His mother bragged, his brothers hugged, and his father made plans to spend the money on a new battery for the radio and a complete overhaul on the old Ford automobile.

Monday morning brought sunshine. The wind had calmed. The gray clouds had gone. Jimmy slipped quietly out of the house and walked toward the little building that housed the rabbit hutch. He entered the room with a heart that ached as much as the heartache that had killed his uncle, or so he thought. It was in writing. Jimmy had killed his pet rabbit to answer his uncle's last request and had thereby fallen into favor of his will.

The boy cried as he carried the rabbit up the hillside. The small white bundle of fur nestled under his arm as the wide eyes gazed at him in seeming admiration and trust. The boy trudged on. He was far atop the hill when he set the little white rabbit on the icy ground. He fully realized that left there, the rabbit would starve or be eaten by its natural enemies of the wild. The boy watched as the little white animal sniffed the air. The rabbit hopped around in a playful circle and looked back at the boy just as the heavy stick caught the back of its head, breaking its neck.

As the years passed, when the family automobiles became newer, when radios were plentiful, when color television brought pictures of the weather front coming down from Canada, they still talked of the day Jimmy killed the rabbit.

Tom T. Hall

A member of the Nashville Songwriters Hall of Fame, Tom T. Hall is known for his vivid characters and narrative strength. Born in 1936 near Olive Hill, Kentucky, he has had a long and varied career that includes more than fifty chart hits on forty albums, Grammy and CMA Awards, and over twenty top-ten successes. In 1971 he became a member of the Grand Ole Opry, and has been named Songwriter of the Year and called "the poet laureate of country music." He has also published six books, including a novel, a short-story collection, and an autobiography.

His classic songs include "Old Dogs, Children and Watermelon Wine," "I Love," "The Year That Clayton Delaney Died," and "Homecoming." He has created a solid body of children's music, some notable political-satire pieces, and some of Nashville's rowdiest beer-drinking anthems. His "Harper Valley P.T.A." sold 6 million singles, inspired a movie and a TV series, crossed over to become a number-one pop hit, and became a nationwide sensation.

Hall has been almost as potent as an interpreter. His voice immortalized the bluegrass standard "Fox on the Run," revived chestnuts like "It's All in the Game" and "P.S. I Love You," and originated such country staples as "Song of the South" and "Old Five and Dimers Like Me." He has also forged some remarkable musical bonds, collaborating with Johnny Cash, Patti Page, Earl Scruggs, Dave Dudley, and Bill Monroe.

A national TV celebrity and a notable commercial spokesman of the 1980s, in the 1990s he has become known for his charitable activities, creative-writing workshops, and one-man shows. And through it all he has remained a man of the soil. Today he lives just outside Nashville, Tennessee, where he continues to write songs and stories. You can visit his Web site at www.tthproject.com.

Career Day

★

Robbie Fulks

A feeling of greatness just around the corner has been a constant in my life. It tends to peak—I've noticed it only afterward—just as I am about to go traipsing into a nest of armed criminals or fall into an open manhole. It is a signal, in other words, a malign light blinking a yellow warning, dear dull old Mother Nature's way of portending calamity by inculcating cheer. I have come to rely on it, though a little late. The conviction that "This is going to be great!" plunged me blindly into marriage in the midnineties, and a short while later into the high-tech market. Since the (suspiciously closely timed) collapse of both, I have paid careful attention to all premonitions of personal glory, making sure to stop my ears and run the other way.

Who knows why the emergency systems were down the day my wife, a classically attractive ice sculptress of Mitteleuropean stock, broke the news that she had committed me to appear at a school function in a distant town, to talk at length about the life of a professional musician. Not that I didn't resist such a sickening idea instinctively and immediately—I did. But for my failure to fight the current of positive thinking that later picked me up and buffeted me to an all-too-predictable doom, I can only point feebly to the universally compromised condition of man in these postlapsarian times. The school in question was Prairie Butte High of District 47 in Wheatstraw, Illinois, just over an hour's drive from our place on the north shore of Chicago. One of the deans there was an old family friend, and my wife's giddy tone implied that my own career, rather than those of the upperclassmen, would be the clear beneficiary of my effort and time. She was the soul of salesmanship.

"You'll talk about making records," she said, "and traveling from town to town to perform. You'll explain how the business is structured and how you combine your various income streams—royalties, Web site sales, et cetera."

"I'll do no such thing," I asserted. "You seem to think of my income stream as a freestanding ecological structure, something I can blithely walk away from for hours on end with no effect on the family purse..."

"And you'll be a good role model. The successful, happy, articulate man of the arts."

"Me no like talking in public," I said, trying a new tack. "And I doubt that I have anything of interest to offer teenagers."

"You are a very interesting person," she assured me.

"To you, evidently. To high schoolers, maybe not so much. Have you looked in the trades lately? Fringe country isn't soundscanning with exurban youths, by and large. It seems to appeal exclusively to fifty-something fanzine editors with big stomachs. Mainstream record consumers—'kids' for short—are more interested in...starlets, and black guys with handguns yelling about pussy and that."

"You have songs about pussy," she purred. "Talk about that if you want to. Obliquely. This is the kind of thing I needed but never got when I was in high school." Dropping her hands into the pockets of her work pants, she began a slow rhythmic jiggling of coins and die grinder bits. "*I* never had the opportunity to talk to the great ice artists. I had never *heard* of the Inuit Free-Range Quarries, the National League of Bachelorettes, the Greenland Carnivale. Never thought about the storing or transporting of large blocks of ice, much less simple heartbreak. All I knew was the lust for fame." She brought her eyes down from Polaris and fastened them firmly on me. "No one told me that it would probably never come—and that it didn't matter. No one told me that artists can earn the respect of their peers and a living income without ever gaining an ounce of celebrity. You can work and work and work, all your life, and never be—"

"Okay, stop," I said. "So I'll do a little talk. I'll take some questions. I'll make a pie chart. How long does the presentation need to be?"

"Forty minutes. But you have to do the forty minutes seriatim for five consecutive groups. It's kind of an all-day thing."

To conceal from your wife that your professional life involves doing not very much all day long is a challenge few men can crack. Once the secret is out, it's almost impossible to weasel out of any worthy commitments she might drum up on your behalf. But the real reason I caved was that Career Day appealed to my vanity. Lives there a nearsighted, saggy-jowled old fool who does not flatter himself to suppose that his example might lead some grateful novice to the light? Add to that the prospect of a captive audience of delighted adolescents, which holds a dizzying, archetypal power for any musician, and you have a potent cocktail. When Career Day dawned, my pie chart was in the back of the car. Cheer was regnant.

Prairie Butte High was a drab cuboid situated on a gently

raised stretch of cow country, thirty miles northwest of Chicago's farthest bedroom suburb. Inside, the sights and smells of my own high school rose immediately from the dead. There it all was again, the fierce mammal energy, the gray hallways vibrating with the metal echo of locker doors and bells, the smell of something like potted meat, the provocatively attired girls a guy like me could never bed, though now with added disincentives to try. The boys were dressed casually in jeans and khaki, as in my day, but with far more stylish cuts and colors than the Jimmy Carter School for Slobs used to allow. Whether or not high school fashion is destiny, the look stuck to me; I was wearing frayed Levi's and a flannel shirt.

Terry, the dean, had a red lapel sticker ready for me, reading MUSICIAN.

"We are so thrilled to have you here!" She beamed behind slim-framed eyeglasses, a cordwood-stack of binders balanced in the crook of her arm. "Mr. Legg, our social studies teacher, is such a fan—he has an alternative country band too! He wants to meet you, if you can spare a moment after fifth period. Now, we have you set up in room 1355, down this hall, last door on the left. Oh—Mr. Stritch, your name tag and packet!" A muscled figure in pinstripes, about my age, stopped in passing. He gamely accepted and applied his INVESTMENT BANKER tag. "You're in 1580 today, just down—oh, by the way, meet our famous musician, Robbie Fulks!"

Stritch pumped my hand briskly. He glanced down at my sticker and up at me, quickly and without pleasure. "Pleased," he grunted, and power-fled down the corridor.

"Well, banking." I smiled conspiratorially at Terry. "That should be quite the draw with the young 'uns. I always forget—was it Roth IRAs or grunge that was big in Seattle fifteen years ago?"

"You're so different!" She smiled back in encouragement. "We're delighted you made time in your busy schedule to join us."

Heading down the hall, I caught some other name tags: exterminator, systems analyst, patent attorney, hairdresser. My wife was right. There was a rich lode of useful experience on tap here at Prairie Butte. To see it given up freely to those still damp from the chrysalis swelled my heart, and spurred my self-confidence. I was going to come alive in 1355! For mine was a story with a moral to gladden young adults everywhere: a life goal didn't need to be a life sentence. Patent attorney? Personally, I'd take Leavenworth.

I had intended to make a splashy entrance: throwing open the classroom door, raising a fist, bellowing, "For those about to Rock...I salute you!" But on entering the room, something in the air, a wetly palpable anomie, struck me hard. A big empty desk, a blackboard, an open window, and near it a computer-generated image of a branching tree festooned with photos of chefs, medical professionals, sleekly dressed business-men. Twenty or so kids sat in neat rows, compliantly frozen.

"You're here for the musician?" I said. A few doleful nods. I crossed briskly to center front and clasped my hands together. "So." Letting my gaze fall meaningfully around the rows— connecting, connecting—I leaned casually against the desk. Like the tuned-in TV and movie teachers of the seventies (Conrack, the White Knight), I strove with body language to express a jazzy informality, a wideness of spirit.

"So. My name's Robbie, and I'm here to tell you what could happen if you decide to pursue music as a career. I've done it for twenty-one years now—written it, recorded it, performed it. You might ask: what notable successes have I enjoyed?" If I knew my youngsters, they were asking themselves just this.

"It all depends on how you define 'success,'" I continued. "Though none of you has ever heard of me, by certain measures I *am* successful. I own my house. I have a nice family. Sales of my records are modest but sustaining. I have made a lot of them, and will continue to.

"Granted, some of my colleagues here at Career Day make more money, have better cars and houses, and so on. They may not get to travel all over the country and jump around onstage and play hot guitar solos—but they may not want to. Doing music on a lower-than-celebrity level is tough work. It can test the spirit. For better or worse, though, that's the level where ninety percent of us in the business find ourselves. Making your living at music makes for an awfully strange journey. But I am here to tell you, it can be done!"

A couple soft coughs. Two boys sitting close to me, wearing identical black shirts with a picture of something like an arachnid corkscrewed around a spear, were wide-eyed with respect.

"I can't help but remember when I was at your age." That sentence, delivered into the rearview mirror on the drive here, seemed *de rigueur* for a Career Day address. "I had no goals. I never thought of sacrificing or building for the future. All I thought about was playing the guitar. Okay, meeting girls and getting high, those might have been tied for second. Ha, ha, ha. But mostly, guitar. The chord was my shepherd—ha!" The "getting high" part was a risky move, but the White Knight would have taken it. The arachnid twins showed approval, bouncing their legs and nodding.

"Now, the music I do is—hold your applause—country. That was the family tradition I was raised in, and in the South, it wasn't necessarily an uncool thing to pick fiddle tunes and sing about the old homestead. My folks started me off and I got the rest from record albums.

"Today, things are very different. For one thing, young people have access to many, many more resources. A recent *New Yorker* article used the phrase 'platform agnostic.' It means that, of all the numerous distribution outlets available today—podcasts, satellite, iTunes—kids are content to go anywhere and everywhere. There is no single, socially anointed outlet for learning about new music. Which is wonderful. Where do you guys find out about new music?"

The direct question stimulated nervous shuffling. Then a girl said meekly, "The radio." Others murmured assent. "Ninety-eight point four," someone said, and a few chuckled in recognition.

"All right," I said. "Theoretically, anyway, you have choices, whether or not you choose to exercise them. Now, this new game, with its proliferation of outlets, is a threat to some of the players, such as record corporations and the upper elite of brand-name performers. Just as with the TV business since the advent of cable and Fox and pay-per-view, the democratization of the music business means less centralized control, and probably most of us will earn a bit less on average for our work. But it also means more consumer choice, and it means that people like me, niche artists who ride around in a van performing for one or two hundred people at a time, have a better shot at expanding and prolonging their careers, as long as they're willing to do a little extra work to promote themselves."

"You go around in a van?" said a young man, his head loaded with curly brown hair and his voice with acidulous disbelief.

"I do. It's not that bad!"

"And you play country music. In..."

"Bars. To put it bluntly. And at weddings, and other places too. Hey, I brought a pie chart!" I lifted the posterboard up onto the chalk tray. It showed that marvel of nature, my income stream, split into categories. "When most 'normal' people—my neighbors or my auditors—find out I'm a musician, the first thing they want to know is: How? How is it possible to have an income when you're not on TV, or ninety-eight point four? I mean, sure, I've been on TV and radio some, but that kind of thing is almost completely irrelevant to making a living. So how do you support—"

"You were on TV?" Curly again. His eyebrows were raised, but they exerted no lift on his lids. "Like what TV?"

"TV shows that routinely promote music released by big labels," I said a little testily. "I was on one, briefly. A label, I mean."

"What was your big hit?" he said.

"As I said, nothing you'd have heard. And now, we return to our pie chart. Here you see performance royalties. BMI and ASCAP are the names of organizations that collect statutory..." And, having dispensed with Curly Pubeskull, I was off on a roll. Like most men, I confess, I am a pushover for a curve, a graph, a vector, anything that converts complex realities into cute 2D shapes, no matter how fundamentally inaccurate. I picked over each pie slice with analytical rigor and care. I laid out the economics of touring. I spoke of the value of commercial work and the relevant unions. I described the publishing industry, touching briefly on the knotted area of digital rights and the as-yet-unknown media of the future. I was Conrack on steroids. When I had finished, I looked at my watch. Since I had walked into the room, eleven minutes had passed.

"Okay, and now I...guess I'll open the floor to questions. Questions? Anyone?" Overhead a ceiling fan whirred. I tapped the desk behind me, to ward off the yawning silence opened by my invitation. Gently, through the open window, there drifted in the idiotic barking of dogs. As the second hand cycled sluggishly, I reflected that a lifetime's experience can be summed up in minutes, easily. You could also do it in a couple of days, with plenty of colorful digressions and character development, and some lively back-and-forth with your listeners. But a fortyminute oral autobiography with only a sprinkling of hostile interruptions turns out to be a tall order.

A brunette sitting toward the back was tugging abjectly at her hair. Other students sat with heads and hands in every possible conjoinment except the one signaling thought. One, the size of an adult dockworker, slept openly. Even the arachnids looked flummoxed.

"Come on," I said. "There must be *something* about my chart or my job that interests someone. Is anyone curious to hear more about getting a record deal? Demoing songs? Scoring an independent movie? Anything at all?" I snuck another look at my watch. Eleven minutes and forty seconds. I was anxiously thinking of ways to fill the rest of the period—doughnuts perhaps, a folk song—and coming to grips with the realization that the content of my story and my White Knight tactics had not gone over as hoped. In fact, I had quite comprehensively bored these people. Had there been fundamental changes in the teen outlook since Jimmy Carter? Or was the thing that had absorbed me for the last two decades considerably less romantic than I had assumed?

But hark: a voice from the gallery! It belonged to the brunette, who had been regarding me with a dim but growing curiosity. Evidently she was fishing for the right words. They now rose to her lips. "What are you going to do . . . when you're *sixty*?"

As a moment, it would have felt more complete punctuated by a burst of group laughter and some pointing. But the girl was patently sincere, and she had expressed a general mood of perplexity in the room.

"Yeah," amplified another girl, "do you think you'll have a big hit by then, or will you still be playing weddings and bars?" The dogs in the distant field had fallen still. I studied the blue lines on the backs of my hands.

"The same thing," I said. "Music in bars. Career Day appearances."

"Oh, you're being sarcastic," Curly observed.

"No, I'm having the time of my life," I said. "I'm just not sure we're getting anywhere. Is anyone here remotely thinking about going into music after graduation?" To my relief, the arachnids' hands shot up. "I *thought* we had two musicians here! Guitar?"

"Yeah," said one.

"What kind of music?"

"Um," said the other. "I don't know what you'd—you know…just…" They looked at each other and put their heads together, trying to come up with a word to describe the kind of music they played. "It's just, normal music. He plays lead. I just started last year."

"This is some species of rock we're talking about?"

The one on the right thought of a helpful referent. "Like Breakbone Fever, or Chimps in Aspic. Just, music. How important is practicing?"

"Very. I mean, I don't know. It depends. I don't know anything about that kind of music. Maybe it's important never to practice."

"How do you write songs?"

"I don't know. Please don't go into music, guys."

"What TV shows have you been on?"

"Normal TV shows."

"Like, what shows?"

"The *Today* show, *Conan*..."

Curly slouched forward, ever so slightly. "You were on *Conan*?" He sounded like David Spade. A less-excited David Spade.

"Yes, I appeared on *Conan* one time when somebody canceled last-minute."

"What was he like?"

"Conan? He was...I don't know, I talked to him for all of thirty seconds."

"How tall was he?" the brunette wanted to know. The class was now hanging on my every word. I wished they were not.

"Tall. My height. Listen, being on a show like that, it's not really as big a deal as you'd think."

"Being on TV is cool," observed Arachnid One.

"Sure," I admitted. "It's cool for your friends and family, a cool thing to watch someone they know. But to do, not as much. You're standing around in a little room for hours on end. It's not that big a deal. Donald Sutherland was the guest the day I was on."

"You don't like Donald Sutherland?" said Curly. "Donald Sutherland isn't good enough? I think Donald Sutherland is pretty cool."

"Donald Sutherland is cool. Forget Donald Sutherland. I'm talking about the romance of TV. It's an illusion. A guy in my band played on *Saturday Night Live* in the nineties. I asked him what it was like. He said it was cold, and people in the cast were mean. There's your TV for you."

"Was Donald Sutherland the host?" Curly was actually sneering.

"I think *Saturday Night Live* is cool," mumbled Arachnid Two. They were starting to form a solid black lump in my near vision.

"Hey, here you are!" said the dockworker, who had woken at some point and opened a laptop. "Look what I found. 'Robbie Fulks was briefly an interesting figure in the mid-1990s Chicago-area "insurgent country" scene,'" he read. "That's pretty cool. You're right here on this Web site."

"It's cool if you like being referred to in the past tense, or as a representative of a movement," I said. "If you think it's a great honor to appear on the Internet."

"I don't know," Curly reflected. "I might just appreciate being referred to at all. Especially if I played music that wasn't popular."

"It's got a song on here!" said the dockworker. And in a moment there was my voice, caterwauling in the little classroom on the prairie. I mean, it was my voice as it was nine years earlier, singing lyrics written five years earlier still, over an orchestration driven by sounds in vogue at least ten years before that. The song dramatized small-town despair, and was written in a Super 8 room during a lonely couple of days between bars. Normal music.

"That's *you* singing?" said the brunette.

"Mm-hmm."

The arachnids, my last best hope, could hold out no longer. They covered their mouths out of politeness and turned from me. Around the laptop, a small group stared raptly at the little machine, as if it were playing a video file rather than an MP3. Perceiving my singing through their ears, I heard an aboriginal yammering. The computer's built-in speaker rendered the recording shrilly remote, as through an Edison cylinder.

"Excuse me," I said. I picked up my posterboard and slipped into the hall. Through the pane in the door opposite me, I spotted a familiar face. Name tag: HAIRDRESSER. She was in the middle of a circle of relaxed, smiling students; she was giving one of them a cut. And there was Stritch, too—in my mind's eye, anyway, and I don't doubt its acuity—doing a 401(k) song-and-dance, and going over like Jolson.

Lowering my face like a penitent, I ducked out a side door, half-circled the building, and trotted down the soft incline to the parking lot. Leaving a populous city for the small staid towns and the country beyond, one feels the enactment of a pleasant shift, the glamour of ideas and organized industry giving way to the bedrock of custom and honest toil. To return is to recall that, for most of us, sparkling ideas and illusions are not as much like idle playthings as they are bread and water. In either direction, the trip offers the blessed false promise of escape.

I would call my wife on my cell phone, telling her they had released me early. That would take care of her. Then, with the wheels spinning beneath me and the countryside filling in with subdivisions and strip malls, I would work on a song in my head. With luck it would prove intelligible to others; and that would take care of me. As for the kids of 1355, they will have to find their own escape route. Let 'em be doctors and lawyers and such.

~~~

Robbie Fulks

Robbie Fulks was born in York, Pennsylvania, and grew up in Virginia and North Carolina. Since 1983 he has lived in and around Chicago. In the 1980s he played guitar for the bluegrass band Special Consensus and taught music at the Old

Town School of Folk Music. In 1993 he started working in Nashville as a country songwriter, and shortly after that began recording country CDs under his name, of which eight have been released to date. He also produces records (Dallas Wayne, the Johnny Paycheck tribute Touch My Heart*) and sings on commercials (McDonald's, Budweiser, Applebee's, and more).*

He has scored one failed sitcom for Fox and a couple terrible films, and worked a little in regional theater. His live-music-and-interview program, Robbie's Secret Country, *airs thrice monthly on XM satellite radio. His writing has appeared on-line and in print publications such as* GQ, Blender, Journal of Country Music, *and the* Chicago Reader, *and has been anthologized in Da Capo's* Best Music Writing *series. You can visit his Web site at* RobbieFulks.com.

How I Stayed a Boy

Tia Sillers

There is something strangely glorious about being an accident—particularly if you're a child with an imagination. Your view of the world is fundamentally altered, forever tilted once you've uncovered how desire and nature came together one early winter's night and ignited a combustion of sorts. I still can't help but be filled with a kind of guilty pleasure, knowing that all it took was a few moments of recklessness to trigger an unintended chain reaction that wound up becoming, well...me.

So it goes that in August of 1939, at the tail end of the Great Depression and on the cusp of World War II, I came into this world: unplanned, breech, two weeks late, and screaming. Born in my parents' bed on a four-hundred acre barley-tobacco farm just north of Ghent Springs, Kentucky, I was the sixth of six daughters born to a very exhausted forty-one-year-old mother and a very disappointed forty-five-year-old father. And, as the years wrote out our lives, the family lore claimed that when I was finally born and my sex became known, my father, after alternately crying and drinking for most of a week, announced that he was changing my name from Claudia Ann to Francine Samantha and that I would henceforth be known as Franky. My father's name, by the way, was Franklin Samuel Owen and, for a while, in addition to Franky, people called me Junior.

It was also whispered that Daddy never slept with my mother again—a highly effective form of self-imposed birth control. I can't help but wonder if believing that my mother was never again held by a passionate, albeit often drunk, man for the rest of her life had some profound effect on my development. Surely there are certain family secrets that are best kept in the dark. In Daddy's defense, for most men, six children, let alone six daughters, is more than enough, and he *was* a sweet drunk.

But even for all of that, there is still something strangely glorious about being an accident. When you're a living, breathing mistake, this world can offer a brilliant sense of freedom. Somehow if you weren't supposed to exist in the first place, you could feel that everything you did in life was pretty much gravy. In my young mind's eye, I could get away with more, because I wasn't quite as there, or really as real, as the rest of the intended or on-purpose beating hearts out there. All of those intentional souls had to watch their step, had to make their days and nights matter, because *they* mattered. God was keeping an eye on them. But not me. I was such an afterthought I didn't even come into this world headfirst like everybody else, and they'd renamed me three times before I was even a month old. It was like my footsteps were less visible in the backyard chicken-scratch dirt, and it wouldn't take much wind or water to wash them away. It was almost like I was half ghost, half child, and that kind of existence helped lead to a life not threatened by solitude.

Still, I was always so thrilled when Daddy would scoop me up and carry me under his arm like a sack of feed, with my legs in the air sticking out behind him. Thrilled when he would take me into town for a new pair of overalls and let me get my hair cut in the chair right next to him at the barbershop, all the men chuckling whenever we walked down the street on the way to the feed store or the soda shop hand in hand. "Here comes Frank Sr. and Junior." And then there were those wonderful nights when my father would tuck me into bed with just a nip of Evan Williams on his breath and ask, "Who loves little Frankie?" And I'd say, all heavy-eyed and smitten, "Big Frank does."

But I wasn't a boy. And that, I guess, was the dark heart of the matter. If I had been, everything really would have been different. With one different chromosome, I would have gone from being an accident to being the long-awaited answer to countless prayers, the son after five daughters, the rain after a ten-year drought. I tried not to look like a girl, not to act like a girl, never let Momma grow my hair long or make me wear a Sunday dress. I kept my skinny knees and elbows scraped from climbing trees and straddling fences. I knew, from an improbably young age, that my family needed a son and I was the closest they were gonna come to it.

My oldest sister Lorraine was almost thirteen when I was born, soon to be long gone with the first boy that talked smooth and held an equivocal sense of promise. The twins, Ruthie and Rose, were ten, Lucille was nine, and Helen had just turned seven, so by the time I was old enough to be aware of my surroundings, my sisters were busy going through what seemed to be a constant coming of age. And every one of them was exactly what I wasn't: one hundred percent woman-child. What started out all pink and giggly had, by the age of fifteen or so, given way to hourglass figures and husky laughs from stealing boyfriends' Pall Malls. It's crazy, looking back now, how they all wanted to be Hollywood bombshells instead of girls from Ghent Springs and I wanted to be a son instead of a daughter.

If I were to give you mental snapshots of each of my sisters they would look like this:

Picture Lorraine, with her long jet-black hair, studying herself smoking a cigarette in the side mirror of Daddy's pickup while trying out lines like "Well, aren't you a picture" and "My lamb, my lamb" all slow and low. She was the breathless one, always biting her lip and batting her eyes.

If there ever was a "sweater girl" to give Lana Turner a run for her money it would have been Ruthie. I can still see her wearing an impossibly tight Sears and Roebuck ecru number with an egg blue scarf around her neck. Still see her swinging on the front porch humming "You must have been a beautiful baby..."

Then there was Rose, in her platform shoes and navy blue sailor shorts, a white shirt tied at the sternum, climbing up the ladder in Curtis Reed's daddy's hayloft to do heaven knows what (me hiding behind the tractor, watching them sneak in).

And speaking of what, what about Lucille leaning on the door of Walter Bradshaw's Plymouth, actually effortlessly saying, "Hey Walter, if you need me just whistle. You know how to whistle don't you?" And Walter swallowing hard, looking at her all torn because he knows how to whistle. Hell, he won the 4-H Club bird-calling contest. He knows how to whistle and he knows it's just a movie line but he wants to hear Lucille Anne Owen say it because if she's playing Bacall that means he's Bogey and...and..."Why you just put your lips together and blow."

Finally, there was Helen—she's the one I followed around the most. I can still see her posing for Hank Cummings's brand-new Kodak camera: her fingers laced behind her head, elbows in the air, eyebrows penciled just so, and a look for the lens that was X-rated. Somehow, she was standing there in that yellow eyelet dress revealing nothing and promising everything.

The truth is, for a kid like me they were fantastic. While the rest of the world watched their starlets in black and white over at the town cinema, I got to witness five femmes fatales all life-sized and in Technicolor. Yes, the Owen sisters were too much and yes, they were destined for trouble, but for me, growing up as a child who wasn't supposed to be there and as a girl who wished she was a boy, all those sisters were a fabulous distraction. They smelled like chocolate malted milkshakes, gardenias, and a pure musky sexiness. They had lovesick pups driving slow past our house at all hours of the night. They had mothers all over town saying "Jesus, Mary, and Joseph."

I must have been almost four when Lorraine quit school and ran off with a could-have-been-minor-league-shortstop-if-it-hadn't-been-for-Pearl-Harbor kinda guy named Howard Housten. Momma told me that they went to California when he joined the navy. In the years Lorraine was gone we got exactly two postcards from her. One showed a black Packard sedan on a muscular winding road cut into the cliffs of Malibu, with a foaming surf, white gold sand, and an impossibly blue sky as a backdrop.

The other card had an all-on-fire neon sign that said *The Boulder Club—BETS FROM A DIME UP! Craps—Twenty One—Roulette.* It was surrounded by a night sky that glowed a crazy electric blue in the distance, like maybe the desert sun had just set. We had no idea where the Boulder Club was and only found out much later that it was in Las Vegas. On the back of both cards she wrote the same thing: *Dear all—Wish you were here. Yours very truly, Mrs. Howard Housten.* Below those words was a huge poppy red lipstick kiss. Lorraine had flown to the moon.

The spring before I entered first grade marked the first time ever that the family wasn't broke. The war was over, the farm had had a few banner years, and suddenly GOD BLESS TOBACCO posters were up in the grocery and the courthouse. Momma and Daddy had finally saved up enough money to be the first people in McClane County to have screens put on their windows. Now, my mother was salt of the earth and she was never one to flaunt, but I do think she held her chin a fraction higher and her back a little less bowed. I do think she even moved us up a few rows in church.

Screens! You can't imagine the magnitude of that simple invention. The luxury of being able to have all the windows open in those mosquito-riddled dog days of August! Somehow, that and a dozen dollars in the coffee can helped forgive everything my father wasn't or wouldn't or couldn't be. My mother loved Frank Sr. more than ever as she stood in the front yard and watched him install that fine mesh wire on all the windows and doors. She must have thought, *Bring on the flies, bring on the crickets, bring on the locusts, Lord. We've got screens.*

You have to understand that up until now, Momma had always been the unfailing realist of the family. She was the bill payer and the penny saver. She was the one who walked the three miles into town at midnight to pull Daddy off the barstool and somehow managed to get him into the bed of our old truck and drive him home. She was the one who believed that life in Ghent Springs was what it was: sometimes interesting, sometimes maddening, sometimes comical, and most often a grind.

Mix up that realism with a dose of fierce Catholic upbringing, and you'll get a hint of the strange amalgamation that Momma was. Her human nature would never quite let her buy into the very Catholic notion that a million rosaries meant answered prayers. She couldn't quite swallow the idea that a lifelong hell-raiser could bargain his way into heaven with a final act of contrition: why worry about being good from the get-go if you're forgiven in the end? All of that body and blood of Christ and incense and ashes and holy water just didn't add up in her brain. She knew in her gut that bad things happened to good people and it was nothing personal. She knew that if she were ever to ask "Why me, Lord?" the most likely answer (if there would even be one at all) would be "Why not?"

Yet she couldn't let it go. Despite all of the things she knew in her head and heart, religion had a way of trumping reality at the end of the day. Kept her glancing in a godly direction and mumbling a prayer with each new rumor that floated around about her daughters or husband. And when you consider everything that was going on in foggy-windowed Plymouths and darkly lit haylofts, when you consider that more nights than not, Frank Sr. was pissing on his boots in the alley behind the Anvil Bar—well, you couldn't really blame her.

But the screens weren't only a momentous occasion in that they represented a rising in local social standing; they also arrived in time to punctuate a line of demarcation. I'd be starting school that fall and my mother would finally, after eighteen years, have a few hours here and there without children or chores. I think she envisioned afternoons with less fortunate "screenless" women, drinking iced tea and mastering the art of needlepoint. For the promising months of May and June 1946, I think she allowed herself to be lulled into an extended moment of suspended reality, sheer fantasy: freedom was waiting just around the bend. She suddenly wore a secret smile and seemed a little more girlish. In a sense, she was brimming with anticipation of living the "good life." I could tell that Momma had begun to believe she was due a little fun.

MRS. HOWARD HOUSTEN, née Lorraine Beatrice Owen, showed up at suppertime on the twenty-third of June, with a basket containing a two-month-old infant she failed to introduce or ever acknowledge. She sat the basket on the kitchen table, reached into her white leather clutch for a cigarette, muttered, "I know, I know...," and stepped out on the back porch to light up. No one said a word. We all must have watched her standing there in the twilight for several minutes before Momma was distracted by the sound of the baby waking up. She cleared her throat and then carefully said, as if reading a script for the first time, "Honey, we're so glad you're back. You can't imagine how much we've missed you." Momma stole a glance at the agitated infant and, in a voice wanting desperately to sound nonchalant, said, as if an afterthought, "And who have we here?" Momma did not reach out to comfort the child.

Lorraine took the time to slowly exhale a lungful of smoke before saying, "It's not Howard's. I hadn't seen him in over a year when I got word he was MIA. It could be Bruce's, but that's done, and Thomas says I can't pursue my career and he won't marry me with a baby on my hip."

Lorraine was now blond, almost twenty—and deadly. When she'd left at sixteen she was sexy but harmless, kind of like ordering a Shirley Temple in a martini glass. But this latest edition of Lorraine was potent stuff, leaner and somehow leggier in a tight dove gray suit and unbelievably high white stilettos. Her hair was teased, sprayed, "done"—and it wasn't going anywhere. Her heavily penciled eyes were those of a poker player, revealing nothing. She had traded her wild coltishness for a horse-broke steely self-restraint, but it wasn't like she'd been broken or tamed by someone else. No, Lorraine had done it to herself. Somewhere along the way she had realized that she could get farther down the road by trading unpredictable heat for a highbrow kind of cool—this new Lorraine could look at you without a trace of hunger or wonder or playfulness and hold it there. You might have to look away, but she wouldn't. Everything about her seemed effortless: everything was on and in place, and somehow, though you were sure it was, it didn't seem fake.

And it was with all of this self-control that Lorraine—who had yet to sit down with us at the kitchen table, who had not taken her jacket off despite the heat, who had, by now, casually picked up her clutch—walked to the opposite side of the kitchen, stood near the doorway to the living room in the front of the house, and said, "I have the late show at the Apache starting in September and Thomas swears we'll be at the Golden Nugget by spring. The hours are going to be pure insanity...."

A car horn interrupted and we were all suddenly as skittish as a herd of deer, every ear alert, but Lorraine showed no reaction and continued her monologue: "So you see it's really quite impossible to raise a baby under such circumstances." And then, like she'd stepped straight out of a movie, she blew us a kiss. She blew us a kiss, turned, and walked out.

I remember running to the window, not the door, and watching the scene unfolding through the screen. It was like I wanted some filter or protection from reality, and the window, being a smaller portal, served that purpose.

There she was, climbing into an unbelievably shiny, silver Cadillac. And there was Daddy, grabbing the car door and refusing to let go, yelling, "Lorraine, now you get your skinny ass back in the house and get that baby. I don't care what kind of spineless son of a bitch you're planning to ride off into the sunset with, but you're not gonna skip out on your responsibility. You brought that child into the world and you're damn well taking it with you...." He was saying all of this as he was running down the drive trying to keep up with the moving vehicle. The car was kicking up chalky dust as it accelerated and began to drag him. My father finally let go a hundred yards from the house, yelling, "Goddamn it, Lorraine. You are not doing this to us."

But she was. And we all knew it. She and What's-his-name were already a mile down the road and they weren't looking back. Daddy spit. Momma, who had been standing in the drive with Ruthie, Rose, and Helen, turned and walked slowly back into the house, her shoulders slumped, her eyes almost closed. I followed her back to the kitchen and watched her run her hands across her face, trying to pull the moment together. She was breathing through her mouth and instinctively reached down to pick up the silent baby, whose enormous eyes were wide open. She began pacing the room, holding the child.

"Momma," I asked. "Are we gonna have to keep the baby?"

"Junior, I don't know," she said.

"Momma, where's the baby gonna sleep?"

"I don't know."

"Momma, what's the baby's name?"

She gave a look that was at first exasperated and then just plain exhausted. "Lorraine didn't say, did she now."

A minute must have slipped by with her just kind of vacantly gazing at the child and I asked again, "Is the baby going to have to stay with us?"

She sighed and said, "I'd say it's looking that way."

As I listened to my mother's resigned response, I was suddenly gripped with a realization: My curiosity wasn't motivated by whether or not I'd be sharing my room or helping to change smelly diapers—those notions didn't bother me much—no, it was out of pure self-preservation. The sex of the baby had yet to be revealed, and I just knew that if that uninvited guest lying in my mother's arms was a male, my days as Frankie Jr. were over. If that child was a boy, I'd be back to being just a plain old girl in no time flat. So I didn't ask any more questions. I figured it would all come out in the wash soon enough. Literally.

My father tucked me in early that night. There was no kiss on the forehead or tousling of my hair. He didn't ask "Who loves little Frankie?" He just shut the door and said, "Get to sleep." Through the wall I could hear Momma and Daddy talking and hashing it out, only halfheartedly fighting—it wasn't like words or a thrown plate would change anything. Then I heard the back door close and the truck start up and knew that Daddy was headed into town to claim a barstool. I think I heard Momma crying, but it might have just been the baby.

WHEN WE all struggled out of our beds in the morning, more than just my father felt hungover; we were all a little sideways from a long, sleepless night. Lucille was rocking the baby in a cradle pulled down from the attic and Rosie was frying eggs when I heard Helen ask, "What kind of name is Dianah? Do we have to call her Dianah?"

"That's the name we found on her birth certificate in the basket," Momma said. What she didn't say was that the space for "father's name" was left blank and the last name of the child was listed as Owen. "Besides, when Lorraine comes back, how would we explain that we changed her baby's name?"

I wasn't even seven yet, but I knew enough to know that Momma's statement was pure fiction; Lorraine wasn't ever coming back, no way, no how. And people changed babies' names all the time—I was a perfect example of that. Normally, I would have pointed these discrepancies out, but at that moment the most unstoppable, self-indulgent smile had overtaken my face. Call her Dinah, Winnie, Lou Lou, Esmorelda; dress her up like the doll she was; put a big pink bow on top of her hairless head; paint her fingers and toes China-girl red—it was all fine by me. The only thing that mattered was that my job was secure. I was still my father's son. There was no new boy coming to live in this family.

I put on my work boots and walked out to the barn to find Senior, which is what I had taken to calling Daddy lately. He was standing in the back of the building by the tool bench and seemed to be unable to decide on the first order of business for the day. I knew he had some cobwebs in his head—that's what he called his hangovers—I also knew he was just plain ticked off at this latest turn of events, so I got to work putting oats in the three horse stalls. For a while, we both shared the early morning cool beneath the old barn roof, saying nothing and doing chores. We were both, in our own way, chewing over fate and faith and luck and life. Daddy broke the silence, calling out, "Junior?"

"Yes, Senior," I said, stepping out of the middle stall.

He smiled a little in spite of himself, walked over to me, put a callused hand on my shoulder, and said, "Promise me something, Frankie. Don't you ever do us like Lorraine or any of the other girls. They're all heartbreakers, every last one of them, and they're gonna walk a hard road. You're not like them. I don't mean you're not a girl—I know you're a girl and one day you'll be a woman—but just you stay you. Keep makin' your old man smile…and for God sakes keep your pants on."

"Yes sir," I said solemnly. And then, just because I looked for any excuse to please him, even though I didn't know what in the world it meant, I said, "I'll keep my pants on."

Tia Sillers

There is absolutely nothing average about Tia Sillers. First of all, she wrote her first hit song right out of college ("Lipstick Promises," with George Ducas). She has the unusual distinction of having "Blue On Black," which she cowrote with her best friend Mark Selby and blues artist Kenny Wayne Shepherd, holding the record as the longest number-one in rock chart history: a whopping seventeen weeks.

A Fine Arts major (UNC–Chapel Hill), this Nashville native has also done pretty well on the country charts. She cowrote Pam Tillis's number-one "Land of the Living" and the Dixie Chicks' megahit "There's Your Trouble." She entered uncharted territory again with the attention-getting ode to living life to its fullest "I Hope You Dance," cowritten with Mark D. Sanders and recorded by Lee Ann Womack. This number-one country hit and Top 20 pop hit has earned a Grammy Award for Best Country Song, the CMA and ACM Awards for Song of the Year, and launched several books. It is used at graduations, christenings, and marriages, and was also used in a video to honor the slain students at Columbine, an honor that Sillers says tops them all.

She doesn't write the way others do, either. She plays guitar and piano well enough to pick out melodies, she says, but writes primarily "in her head."

"I think in a cadence," she says. "Things seem to meter out. When I write a song, it automatically takes a melody in my head."

And if all that weren't enough, she calls herself "indomitably happy." Which just might be the secret to it all.

Whitey Johnson

Gary Nicholson

Whitey Johnson was the first guitar player I ever saw that amazed me, and I always go back to that parking lot in Garland, Texas, when someone asks what made me want to play. It was Labor Day 1963 with the new asphalt oozing a black goo that would rob your flip-flops if you didn't keep moving. My baseball buddies and me were hotfootin' all around the shopping-center carnival, rocking the Tilt-A-Whirl and the bumper cars and ruling the Fun House. Leon Phelps was my ride to the fair. His dad played mandolin in a bluegrass band called the Breakdown Boys—they were all mechanics—that was performing there that day. They played before the Valiants, who mostly covered Elvis, Jerry Lee, Little Richard, and Fats Domino. The Valiants had the perfect look for a combo of their day: powder blue shirts, white dickies, tight black slacks, pointed-toe white loafers, and razor-cut pompadours standing tall. Their outfits were complemented by a matching white Fender Telecaster, Stratocaster, and Precision Bass and beige Fender amps. They were smoking and laughing at each other's dirty jokes the whole time the Breakdown Boys played their set of crippled-up Flatt and Scruggs and Bill Monroe stuff. Leon and I tried to look cool and act like rockers, like we didn't like his dad's band, even lighting up behind the flatbed truck that was the stage while his dad was busy workin' the mandolin and couldn't see us.

About halfway through a tortured "Rocky Top" the Valiants' drummer's girlfriend—picture a very tired Tuesday Weld—came running to the back of the stage and let out with the news that Jimmy Rains, their lead guitar player, had missed his plane back from his grandfather's funeral in Lubbock and would not make the show. The news hit them hard. Leon and I watched their lead singer, Randy, instantly drop his cool, collected James Dean swagger and start pacing around his candy-apple-red '57 Chevy, looking up at the cloudless sky crying, "What are we gonna do, what are we gonna do, we can't play without Jim, he's the only one who knows the songs, we're screwed," on and on.

They really were screwed. Randy did not play an instrument; he only sang and looked dreamy-eyed cool. The bass player, Billy Ray, could only play the patterns that Jimmy had tirelessly trained him to play on twelve songs, and Ron, the organ player, could barely block out three-note chords with his right hand. They had never considered playing any music without Jimmy.

Then Randy lit up with an idea: "Hey, what about that albino dude that Jimmy always talks about being the best picker in town, plays at the Holy Roller church?"

"How do you think we're gonna find him in fifteen minutes?" the drummer asked, shifting his girlfriend on his lap.

"I know his mama is the cook at the Nite Owl—my cousin busses tables over there," said Billy Ray. "Well, get her on the phone quick or we're gonna have to pack up and get outta here 'cause if all these people see us standing around they're gonna want us to play whether we've got a lead guitar player or not, and we're gonna suck," Randy said as he flicked his cigarette away.

So I guess Billy Ray called Whitey's mom and somehow they found him and told him to come on down to the fair, because about twenty minutes later Whitey and his brother came pulling up in an old Ford pickup, a Fender Super Reverb covered with a quilt strapped in the back. It was then that I first realized that Whitey was actually black, 'cause his brother was black. I had never heard the word *albino* and had no idea what that meant, but taking a good look at Whitey you could see that though he was white, he wasn't like all us other white boys. Whitey's hair had a yellowish tint that almost looked dyed, and was real frizzy in small tight curls. His lips were big like his brother's, but his eyes were very light blue with pink eyelids that seemed irritated. He wore his black slacks too short with white socks, black penny loafers with lightning strikes on the sides, and a white short-sleeved shirt with a skinny black tie—a uniform for a side musician. While his brother unloaded his amp and lifted it onto the stage, Whitey put his ear down close to his red Harmony Rocket to check his tuning, asking Ron to give him an E note from the organ. He then quickly adjusted the knobs on his amp, cranking up a healthy dose of treble and reverb. He struck a few notes to test his volume, then turned and looked around for the first time to face the Valiants.

"What you guys usually kick off with?" he asked.

"Let's just do 'Johnny B. Goode' to get things going," said Randy, nervously looking Whitey up and down. "In A."

Whitey leaned into the drummer and threw down strong on the intro exactly like the record. The Valiants jumped in with him and they were rockin', but the guys kept looking at Whitey with half-smiles trying to adjust to his driving rhythm, something they had obviously not experienced the same way before. After the first chorus of "Go, go Johnny, go," they got a little more comfortable and fell into a groove. When the solo came up, Whitey tore into it hard, doing all the Chuck Berry licks everybody was ready for, then stretching out a little, but not so much that it would throw any of them off. He just looked out into the crowd smiling, never looking down at his hands on the neck; it was all so effortless. They played the stock ending and before the cymbal crash died, Randy jumped in, singing "Whole Lot of Shakin' Goin' On" in the same key. After that, Randy introduced Whitey to the crowd, explaining that he had come to sit in for their regular guitar player, who had missed his flight.

"Let's have a big hand for him, y'all: Whitey Johnson," Randy said, and there came some scattered applause.

"Not quite white enough," we heard someone holler from the middle of the crowd. I was up close to the side of the flatbed-truck stage and couldn't really see where the voice was coming from, but a bunch of people turned around and looked in that direction. I realized it was some guys with letter jackets and burr heads who were drunk and lookin' to make some trouble.

Randy had enough sense to jump right into "Gonna tell Aunt Mary 'bout Uncle John, said he had some misery but he's having lots of fun" à la Little Richard. The troublemakers were laughing and moving around with their girls sorta but not really dancin' and everything seemed cool for the moment.

Whitey was looking at the guy he was pretty sure must have hollered the "not white enough" stuff, and the way the guy looked back at Whitey made it very obvious that he was the one and there could be more of his racist bullshit to come any minute. Whitey smiled a cold smile till the tune ended, then he turned to the drummer.

"Just give me a strong backbeat," I heard him say. Then he turned to the bass player and organ player and said, "You guys just lay out for a while—I gotta do this." He reached down and turned the volume all the way up on his amp and went into the riff of "I'm a Man" by Muddy Waters. It got everybody's attention quick. People who were playing all the sucker games down the side strip of the fair started making their way to the stage, along with the kids getting off the Ferris wheel and bumper cars that were nearby. Whitey had stepped up to the microphone and was singing, "I'm a man, I spell M-A-N," and glaring hard into the face of the loudmouthed letterman. The groove was so heavy and undeniable, with one huge distorted electric guitar and backbeat drums. Thinking back now, I'm sure none of the folks at the little shopping-center fair in Garland, Texas, 1963, had ever heard anything even resembling what Whitey was laying down. It was acid rock before acid, Hendrix before Hendrix; his semi-hollow body Rocket was howling feedback and Whitey played with it, holding the guitar close to the amp to get the wildest possible electric moans. The sounds he was making were as if he were up in the kid's face yelling at him. He then looked hard at the smart-ass and turned his smile into a stark stare that said *You should be ashamed of yourself, son.* The kid looked very uncomfortable, red in the face and embarrassed.

Whitey's presence expanded before us; he seemed to get physically larger some way when he played a long, mean, dissonant solo. He sang the last verse and ended by taking his guitar from around his neck and holding it next to the speakers to get the loudest feedback yet, then leaned his guitar against the amp and turned the reverb all the way up. He just stood there and glared awhile at the red-faced redneck kid before he reached behind the amp and turned it off to let the sound slowly fade, finally giving some relief to the amazed crowd. Everyone erupted into applause with shouts and whistling while the Valiants just grinned and stared at Whitey for a while before Randy jumped to the mic and announced in his best show-biz voice that they would take a fifteen-minute intermission. It was obvious that Randy couldn't handle following Whitey's outrageous performance with more lame cover tunes.

After they put their instruments down and climbed off the truck-bed stage, the guys came over to Whitey and started praising his playing and thanking him for saving the day. I was standing off to the side watching Whitey show Randy his guitar and tell him what kind of strings he used when a loud voice came from behind me.

"If that little white nigger wants to start some shit, he's come to the right place." Everyone turned to look in my direction at the same time, and I looked behind me to see a big ol' Hoss Cartwright–looking dude taking slow and deliberate steps toward Whitey.

"I saw you lookin' at my little brother like you want some trouble while you were makin' all that racket up there, and I'm tellin' you to git your shit and git while the gittin's good before I bust you upside the head with your piece-of-shit guitar." The words roared out of his fat face.

"Wayne, you got no business coming back here trying to start shit," said Randy, moving in front of Whitey. "This guy's doing us a big favor sittin' in for Jimmy. We couldn't have played without him. Besides that, he ain't done nothin' to you or your little brother."

"Well I just don't like the smart-ass look on his face, anyway. What are you, boy—black or white? If you're white you need to quit ridin' around with niggers, and if you're black, you need to stay with your own kind." Wayne's big voice was not so loud now that he knew no one was gonna side with him, but he had to keep talkin' his shit anyway.

"I guess I'm black and I'm white too," said Whitey. "Nothin' I can do about it, but it ain't nothin' but skin, man, and I sure don't need no more name callin'." He was closin' up his guitar case and winding up his cord. "Guess I'll see you good folks on down the line—it was fun makin' a little music with y'all."

"Hey, Whitey, you're not leavin', are you? We gotta do another set," Randy had a desperate tone in his voice.

"Oh, you guys will do all right without me. I think I've played about everything I know already." Whitey was climbing into the truck; his brother had already loaded up the amp. I watched Randy walk over and put some money in Whitey's shirt pocket and tell him thanks again. As we watched them drive away, everybody looked over at big ol' Wayne and just shook our heads. He mumbled something nobody understood as he walked off. The Valiants didn't make an attempt to play another set. The evening's entertainment closed out with another set by the Breakdown Boys, a repeat of the set they had done earlier in the day—they only knew twelve songs. Leon and I went back to hangin' around the girls at the Fun House.

That was my first time hearing Whitey play, and I couldn't stop thinking about it. I was so inspired by his performance that I made up my mind to really try to learn more, but as I started taking lessons I realized that what he had done that day was far beyond the reach of any teacher I could find, or any scales I could practice, or licks I could pick off of records. He was putting himself into the music in a way that I wouldn't see again until I saw Hendrix the first time, about six years later.

With Whitey it was all about feeling. He had honed a sound that blended all the styles of his heroes—T-Bone Walker and the three Kings: B.B., Freddie, and Albert, with a strong dose of some kind of surf-guitar weirdness that no one around the Dallas area was hip to yet. His performances in local clubs became the thing all the musicians were talking about. He could be a wild one, doing everything from playing behind his back and over his head, to playing with his teeth, falling to his knees, lying on his back slidin' across the stage. Anything you'd ever seen any guitar trickster do, Whitey would do it with a manic, fun-loving smile, making it look so easy.

The story came around after Whitey's death that he had seen Hendrix play in Vegas with some lame lounge act, a gig he had to take while Little Richard wasn't working. Whitey went there every night after hours when he got off his own gig at midnight. Apparently he got to be friends with Jimi and learned everything he could from him. Anyway, it was a wonderful surprise to hear that first Hendrix record and begin to understand a little about where Whitey had been coming from.

About two weeks after the fair moved on, Leon came by the house one Sunday afternoon and told me he had heard that Whitey would be playing at the Pentecostal church over on the east side of town for a fund-raiser for a new building. He got this information from Billy Ray's cousin, who worked at the Nite Owl, where Whitey's mom was a short-order cook. We had no way to get there except to ride our bikes because we sure couldn't ask our parents to give us a ride to the black part of town to sneak into a church. It would be a longer bike ride than we would usually consider, but by now I had a few more guitar lessons in me and I was ready to go check out Whitey again and see what I might pick up. Leon and I took off right after supper, telling our parents that we were going bowling and would be home by ten. We got to the church a little early, so we stopped in the 7-Eleven and got a couple of Fudgsicles and cruised the area for a while. It felt a little dangerous for us white boys to be riding through the black neighborhood. We got a few long looks from some kids playin' basketball at the school, and we heard someone holler, "Where you goin', whitey?" after we rode on by.

Leon laughed and said, "Yea, it's whitey, goin' to hear Whitey."

We circled back around to the church and watched people walkin' in for a while until the preacher drove up in his old green Oldsmobile. We were surprised to see Whitey get out of the backseat and come around to open the trunk. He pulled out a new-looking gray guitar case and started walking in behind the preacher. At this point we made our move to get a little closer to the church, figuring we would let the service start and then sneak inside in the most inconspicuous way. But when I saw Whitey walkin' in with that case I couldn't keep myself from pedaling on up and knocking my kickstand down as I coasted in, so I could walk right in behind them. When I realized what I'd done, I fell back a little so they wouldn't notice me and sat in a back pew.

When Whitey opened the case I was amazed. Now I know that it was a Gretsch White Falcon, the top-of-the-line model that I would later see played by Crosby, Stills, Nash and Young, but that night it looked like the guitar that Michael the Archangel would play if called down from heaven on a special rescue mission for the Eastside Church of the Pentecost. The White Falcon had all-gold hardware, including tuning keys, bridge, Bigsby tailpiece, volume and tone knobs, and of course the fine FilterTron dual-coil hum-canceling pickups. The sparkling gold binding on the body and the neck and the snap-on pad on the back made it one of the most over-the-top flamboyant, but classy, electric guitars ever made.

I watched Whitey find a chord and plug into that same Super Reverb he had used at the fair. He turned on the tremolo and got that great Pop Staples shake going with a heavy alternating thumb rhythm. The preacher smiled and said, "Praise the Lord, Whitey, I believe that'll work just fine."

Whitey then sat down in a chair behind the podium holding the magnificent instrument and smiling at the folks as they found their seats. I couldn't take my eyes off him. With no volume on he was making some chords up and down the neck I had never seen before, maybe hearing some melody in his head, and I was fascinated. Then the organist came out and began to play "Doxology" and then "In the Garden" with Whitey quietly chording along. By now, Leon had made his way into church and found me in the back pew. He was a little mad at me for taking off without him and he said we should always stick together in case there was any trouble. But nobody ever gave us much of a second look, and I never felt unwelcome. I did feel out of place, like I was stepping into their world without an invitation, but it wasn't them making me feel that way. The truth is, if anybody had asked me what I was doing there, I would have probably come right out with "I'm here to watch that man play guitar!"

Reverend Eugene Davis got the service under way with a prayer and then made a few announcements regarding the building fund. He gave a brief sermon that didn't sound much different than the usual things we heard at our Baptist church, but when the music started everything changed. Reverend Davis's sister, Marvelle, made her way to the pulpit shaking a tambourine and humming a tune under her breath. When she finally got her 300-pound frame up the steps and turned to face the congregation, she opened her mouth to reveal all her teeth, white ones and gold ones, and let out with a long, sustained soulful vibrato that exploded into a fast-rockin' two-beat version of "Jesus Gonna Be Here Soon." The organist, who had been playing so quiet and reverently, was now kicking the bass pedals in a hard-drivin' pattern that moved everyone to stand up and shout and shake and wave hands in the air and sing out loud. There were more battered tambourines and some cowbells and shakers made from Coke cans filled with dry beans and duct-taped on the ends. Everybody had something to rattle or beat on, and everybody was up on their feet moving. Except, of course, Leon and me. We just sat in a back pew, never daring to get too close to the action. But I did find myself scootin' around the room with my back to the wall so I could zero in on Whitey's hands, which held all the salvation I had come for.

I remember talking to Leon that night while we were biking back home about Whitey's playing in church. Leon was saying he wasn't so impressed, because Whitey didn't do any of the flashy stuff he had done at the fair. But I was even more impressed with Whitey for not stepping out and drawing attention to himself. He just played the hymns and accompanied the singers, keeping himself in the background with a respectful reverence that seemed right for playing in church. He was never too loud, with a sweet tone and that beautiful pulsing tremolo. Besides that, he played a lot of chord voicings and changes that I had never heard before, that were beyond the usual rock 'n' roll and blues we were all used to, and I could feel his depth and soulfulness. The other thing that struck me that night, that I never brought up to Leon, was how much more black Whitey was in church that night with all his people around him. I guess I hadn't thought much about it, but the only other time I had seen him had been onstage with some white boys, and the Valiants were really white. There in the middle of the congregation, laughing and carryin' on and makin' music, there was no mistaking Whitey's race, and it made me wonder what it must have been like for him, having the disability of being white.

The summer days kept dragging by for me. I was mowing yards and helping Leon with his paper route, and trying to get a little better on the guitar. I was taking lessons at the Music Mart from Don McCord, who had once played with Bob Wills and had pictures on the wall to prove it. He had me playing "San Antonio Rose" and "Faded Love," and I was taking him Beatles records hoping he could show me some stuff that might impress the girls. He told me one day that Whitey had gone on the road with Bobby "Blue" Bland and they were gonna work in Vegas and then tour Europe. He said everybody was really talkin' up Whitey, like he was the best around, and it made me proud that I'd seen him play a few times and that he was from our little town.

At my guitar lesson two weeks later I got the news. Whitey had been in a horrible car wreck on the road with Bobby Bland. The driver (Buzz Brown, sax) was in the hospital with a concussion and the front passenger (Kenny Keys, keyboards) broke three ribs and his left arm. Whitey broke his right leg. He was back in Garland staying at his mother's house after seeing Las Vegas, London, Paris, Amsterdam, Switzerland, and who knows what else. We heard all about it from Billy Ray's cousin over at the Nite Owl. Whitey's mom had postcards he'd sent tacked up in the kitchen—so proud of him.

With Whitey off the road, he started playing all the time in church. In addition to the Sunday and Wednesday night services, there were Friday night fish-fry fund-raisers for the new addition, which would be a Sunday-school room. I kept saying I was gonna go to another service, but Leon's dad had found out about us and told Leon never to go back. He said it wasn't because he had anything against blacks; he just thought we might be asking for trouble, that they might think we were making fun of their religion. Besides that, his dad said, we weren't members of that church, and why didn't we just go to our own Church of Christ service. We didn't have a comeback for that one. I thought about going by myself, but it was pretty scary to be biking alone through an all-black neighborhood in those days, even if your destination was church. Besides, it was almost five miles, which seemed like a lot at age thirteen on my hand-me-down bike. Anyway, I never made the trip again. I'd give anything if I had.

The rest of this story is still so unreal to me that I picture it as a movie or a nightmare or a lie someone told that got all stretched out of control in the telling and the retelling. Anyway, with Whitey's mom as a source, this is what happened. Whitey loved to play the beautiful White Falcon that he played in church. The guitar had been left to the church by Otis Reeves, a regional gospel singer who performed with his two daughters for years around North Texas, doing shows with such well-known artists as the Staples Singers and the Mighty Clouds of Joy. When Whitey had his accident, Reverend Davis offered to let him keep the guitar at his house and bring it to the Sunday and Wednesday night services. But Whitey didn't feel good about taking that expensive instrument out of the church, afraid that it could get stolen or something might happen. So Whitey would get a ride to the church with his mom as she was going to the Nite Owl, and he would limp into the reverend's office and play all day long. His leg was in a full white plaster cast, and he was movin' slow on his crutches, so he would just sit there practicing scales and playing along with the radio, and sometimes a few folks from the choir would stop in and they would do a little rehearsal for the Sunday service. This all worked out great until Whitey's mom got moved to the late shift, twelve midnight till nine in the morning. At that point Whitey lost his ride and he went a few weeks without playing the White Falcon. But one Thursday evening Whitey decided he really wanted to play and he was willing to just lie down on the Reverend's couch and take a little nap if he got tired. His mom would stop by and pick him up on her way home in the morning.

Whitey's mom said that when she dropped him off at the church that evening she came in for a while, and Whitey played some hymns for her. She said he was complainin' about his bad leg so she made him take some of the pain medicine the doctor had prescribed. She said he didn't want to take it 'cause it made him too drowsy to play, and that's what he was there to do. But he did take the medicine, and that further explains why he never woke up when the fire started.

I had never heard of the Klan before Whitey's death. I didn't know they existed. Later, when I see films of them in their white hoods burning crosses, raisin' hell in the name of God, I would try to imagine what might have taken place the night they torched Eastside Pentecostal. They didn't know Whitey was in there, but it's still unimaginable to me that anyone could be so full of hate that they would destroy a sweet little harmless church where people liked to smile and dance and sing worship to God. How could they justify it? Wouldn't they reason that their own White God would be a bit disappointed? It's the kind of ignorance I'll never understand. Two of the officers on the scene tried to promote the theory that it could have been some drunk teenage pranksters daring each other into some senseless vandalism that got out of hand, but none of the congregation was gonna buy that; everyone knew it was the Klan.

At least whoever did the torching would have had no way of knowing Whitey was there asleep in Reverend Davis's office—

not that it would have stopped them, but hopefully no one actually intended for him to be trapped in the flames, unable to hobble away fast enough from the thick black smoke he was inhaling, too slowed down by his full-length plaster cast to get out the office door before the flames reached the adjacent storage closet where the lawnmower and gasoline were kept. They said it was the explosion of the gas can at about four in the morning that woke up the neighbors who called the fire department.

No one really knew exactly what happened to Whitey. They say when the fire trucks got there, his body was burned beyond recognition, with his charred white cast smoldering. I never let myself imagine how he might have suffered. I've heard that sometimes when sleeping people die in fires, they might not even wake up, that they just inhale the smoke and pass out and it's over and they don't have to feel the torturous burns while trapped in flames unable to run. I like to imagine that Whitey might have gone out in his sleep like that, and left his body to float above the blaze, looking down on his flesh melting with the flaming White Falcon, witnessing his own cremation with the beautiful instrument at the most holy place he knew, then easing off to heaven. But then I think about the gas can exploding, and how it must have woke him up, and I go back to picturing all kinds of horrible scenes.

I had to go there as soon as I heard about it, I had to see whatever was left of the church and say goodbye to Whitey some way. It took me a while to get up the courage to ask my dad to drive me, but I guess he could tell how much it meant—he just walked on out to the car. On the way there, he told me as much as he knew about the Klan and their activities. He said he had a Masonic friend who was a detective in Dallas and he was gonna talk to him about an investigation. My dad rarely cursed, but I remember him saying, "Somebody's gotta stop those assholes."

When we got there we just sat in the car for a while and looked over the scene. The arched front entrance of the little white-frame church was slouching down humiliated, its scorched doors standing open. It appeared that the arsonist had broken through the stained-glass window closest to the pulpit to start the blaze. The podium and steps for the choir were collapsed and reduced to ashes. Reverend Davis's office, where Whitey had been, was just gone. The gas can exploding had left nothing but black on black charcoal and a blown-out metal desk to reveal that an office had once been there.

Dad was saying we should just go on and leave and was turning the ignition when I overheard one of the officers say something about a melted guitar. I asked my Dad to give me a moment, and I got out and walked slowly up to the still-smoldering rubble at the back of the church. I saw the gold hardware glittering before I saw anything else, then as I stepped through the ashes I could make out the neck. I stood there awhile and took it in. The White Falcon was a charred and twisted mess with blistered paint making ugly black bubbles on what was left of its body. The thick plastic of the pickguard was melted over the gold pickups, and the Bigsby tailpiece was loose with a few broken strings waving. The neck, with its ivoried fret markers intact, was broken where it joined the body and pointed away. The headstock, with its fancy gold tuning keys, was so incinerated that the keys were just lying there, blackened but still attempting to shine. I looked up to see if the cop was watching before I slipped one into my pocket.

I've still got it.

Gary Nicholson

*Gary Nicholson is a multiple number-one-hit songwriter,
a two-time Grammy-winning producer, a world-traveling
performer, recording artist, and session guitarist. In 2006 he
was nominated to the Nashville Songwriters Hall of Fame.*

*Over four hundred of his songs have been recorded in various
genres, including country, rock, blues, folk, bluegrass, and pop,
by such diverse artists as B.B. King, Garth Brooks, Fleetwood
Mac, Bonnie Raitt, Ringo Starr, Willie Nelson, Etta James,
John Prine, the Dixie Chicks, Stevie Nicks, Emmylou Harris,
Keb' Mo', George Jones, the Neville Brothers, Waylon
Jennings, Del McCoury, Guy Clark, and so many more.*

*In addition to his Grammy-winning records with Delbert
McClinton, who has recorded twenty-five of his songs, he
has produced records for the Judds, Wynonna, Pam Tillis,
T. Graham Brown, Chris Knight, and others. His songs have
been included in many major motion pictures and on television.
Gary and his wife, Barbara, live in Nashville, Tennessee,
and have four sons. You can visit his Web site at www
.garynicholson.com.*

Cybersong

Bobby Braddock

Dear Glamnash:
I enjoyed our little IM chat last night. Like I said, I'm not in the habit of going to singles chat rooms. I'm not in search of a mate—there are two or three people I go out with occasionally—but I'm certainly open to knowing new people.

As I told you last night, I teach history at Abraham Baldwin Agricultural College, locally known as ABAC, in Tifton, a small town in South Georgia. I'm 41 and divorced, have a twelve-year-old son who lives with his mother in Atlanta.

How about exchanging pictures. With a screen name like Glamnash, you must be pretty hot. Ha. Do we tell each other our real names?

Take care,
Agprof

Dear Agprof,
Let's don't exchange pictures. How we look, that sort of thing is superficial. I'm not saying that *you* are superficial, but I think it's nice for people to get to know each other from the inside out. Too

often, it's the other way around...we like the exterior, only to find disappointment with the interior. And we've already exchanged names; you're Agprof and I'm Glamnash!

I am very interested in history; I read history all the time. Do you have a specialized field, i.e. American, world, ancient? And what are your other interests, hobbies, etc.?

I told you I have a modeling agency in Nashville, hence the screen name. Although I'm thirty-seven, I still do some modeling myself. I was married five years and I've been divorced six years, no children but I just love kids.

Okay, Mr. Agprof. Tell me more about yourself.

Your friend to the north,
Glamnash

Dear Glamnash:

Well, ex-cuse *me* for being shallow! Ha. No, you're right about getting to know each other on the inside first. But I'm not going to tell you that I'm an ugly man. I don't want you to think I'm some nerdy-looking professor.

OK, I teach U.S. History. I love to read, naturally...the same old American history over and over, but also fiction, especially American literature from the 1920s and 1930s, such as F. Scott Fitzgerald, Sinclair Lewis and Thomas Wolfe. I'm a film buff and like to watch videos and DVDs while I'm doing my two miles on the treadmill (I'm a big fan of the old Alfred Hitchcock movies). I *love* music: classic rock from high school days like Styx and the Eagles, but in the past few years I've really gotten into *country* (red flag? Ha!) My favorite is Alan Jackson. My hobby? Playing my old Martin guitar and writing songs, country songs. And I'm not even a country boy; I was raised in Atlanta. Marietta, actually, just north of Atlanta.

By the way, you write a really good letter. No clues about what you look like? Hair color? Height?

OK, it's time to feed my dog somebody's homework, ha. Look forward to hearing from you if you get the chance to write.

Your cyberpal,

Agprof

Dear Agprof,

If you're wondering why I haven't written in a few days, it's because I've been in a state of shock. I did write you once, but luckily we're both on AOL, so I managed to unsend it. I didn't want to sound ridiculous.

Okay, here goes. First, I love American history; I'm just finishing the John Adams biography by David McCullough and I'm starting one about Benjamin Franklin by H. W. Brands. My favorite book of all time is *Look Homeward, Angel* by Thomas Wolfe!!!!! Can you believe that? But wait, Agprof, there's more. I love the Eagles but I too now love country, and my brother knows Alan Jackson—he built his swimming pool!!!!! You may think I'm making all this up, LOL. But I'm serious. What are the chances of this?

I have no doubt that you're nice looking. You want to send me a picture so bad you can't stand it LOL. And you wanted a few hints about me? FYI I was voted best looking female at Hillsboro High School in Nashville and I am exactly the same weight now that I was then. Feel better? And I'm a strawberry blonde and five foot seven.

Your turn, Bubba.

Glamnash

P.S. I really like the old Hitchcock films too, especially *Psycho*.

Dear Glamnash:

Actually, this is pretty amazing, isn't it!? So tell me: on what long trip did John Adams take a family member along, who did he take

and at what time of the year were they traveling? And just curious,
you tell *me,* what are your politics and your religion?

In utter amazement,
Agprof

Dearest Agprof,
Well, obviously you're the teacher giving me a test, or, more
frankly stated, you're the detective giving me a lie detector test.
Okay. John Adams took his son John Quincy with him to Europe
and they sailed in the dead of winter...which proves nothing,
I could have run to the library to look it up. But why? What
would be the point? Why would I be trying so hard to impress
you? Maybe I should send you a picture of me, I'm definitely not
chopped liver.

Okay, Ag man, my politics? I'm an independent, I probably
vote Democratic more, but sometimes I vote Republican too.
Religion? I was raised a Southern Baptist and still consider myself
a Christian, though I don't go to church regularly. So if that doesn't
match up with you, what are you going to do, stop e-mailing me? LOL

As I roll my eyes,
Glamnash

Hold on there, Glamnash!
Hope I didn't make you mad. Sorry if I sounded cynical. I *am*
amazed, your politics and religion are identical to mine, even down
to the backsliding Southern Baptist!

Okay, we've got to meet. May I drive up to Nashville this next weekend and take you to lunch? We could meet at a restaurant in broad
daylight, just in case you're afraid that I'm the Georgia Strangler, ha.

Listen, why don't we talk about this on the phone...break the
ice...and if you feel good about it, just tell me when and where

to meet you. My daytime phone number is below. And my name is Kevin Babcock (so now you know, ha!).

In anticipation.

Agprof

Dear Agprof,

No, no, no. You're breaking the rules with the name and the phone number. I don't even want to think about them. But yes, I would love for you to drive up to Nashville to meet me. That would be so cool. We'll talk about John Quincy Adams, Thomas Wolfe, Alfred Hitchcock, the Eagles and country music. This coming Saturday would be perfect. At noon. There will be a little safety factor involved, with which I'm certain you will concur: My brother will be along, but he'll leave if and when I tell him to. You may be sorry you asked me to meet you, LOL.

You will be coming into Nashville on I-24. When you start getting close to the city, look for the Haywood Lane exit; the next one after that is the exit you take, Harding Place. Heading west on Harding Place, you'll come to a busy intersection at Nolensville Road. Keep going west on Harding Place for over a mile, and you'll see a convenience store and strip mall on the right. Just before the convenience store is a little restaurant called Mama Mia's. It's a really good Italian restaurant, and we'll meet you there. If you don't like Italian food, let me know, and I'll give you some other directions. As I told you, I am a strawberry blonde, five foot seven, and to be honest, I look like a slightly older Britney Spears (if she were a strawberry blonde). My brother is about my height, has real closely cropped hair, slightly graying, and a beard about the same length as his hair, and he's very muscular (so don't try anything, LOL).

Let me know, ag guy!

This is so weird but so-o-o COOL!!!!!!!!!!

Glamnash

P.S. If you have a CD of some of your songs, maybe my brother could give it to Alan Jackson.

P.S. Again. Please confirm that this is on for Saturday, and please describe yourself.

Glamnash!
I am so danged excited. I probably shouldn't do this, but I'm going to take you up on your Alan Jackson offer. I'll be bringing a CD with three original songs, and you should listen first and be the judge of whether your brother gives it to Alan or not.

I've been to Nashville several times and have a pretty good idea where you're talking about. I think it's just before the I-65 intersection.

OK, I'm about 5'6", not extremely obese but a little pudgy, a tad bald with reddish hair in a ponytail. Hey Glamdoll, I'm messin' with you. I'm actually just under six feet, I weigh what I'm supposed to weigh and my full head of hair is medium brown and curly, covering the tip top of my ears. My eyes are blue. I'll be wearing a bright red shirt so you can't miss me.

I'm planning on having lunch with you, but I don't have to be back to Tifton until late Sunday night (about a seven hour drive?) so if we find each other irresistible, who knows? Ha! *Just in case*.... I've made reservations at a nearby Holiday Inn and I'm bringing along a nice suit. Maybe, just maybe, someone will want me to take her to dinner at a fancy restaurant and spend the night in Nashville.

SEE YOU AT MAMA MIA'S, SATURDAY AT NOON!

The agman cometh,
Agprof

P.S. I drink in moderation, I don't smoke cigarettes and I haven't used marijuana in years.

Hey you, Agprof,

Why, of course you're a social-drinking non-smoking reformed pothead. Just like me!!! Honestly. I think we're so similar that we'll hate each other, LOL. No, not really. I think it's wonderful.

Don't forget that Nashville is in the Central Time Zone, so noon my time is one o'clock Georgia time.

Big guy, I cannot wait to see you. Mama Mia's, Saturday at noon.

Love,

Glamnash

P.S. Please drive carefully.

Dear Glamnash:

What a day I had in Nashville. I thought I'd share my impressions with you. I get to Mama Mia's about 11:55...I go inside and look around...I get a table...I look around...I walk around...I even see a couple who could *possibly* fit your description. "Are you expecting someone from Georgia?" I ask. No luck. I go back to my table and sit and wait...and wait...and wait...then I start walking around the restaurant again.

Over in the corner sat an Asian boy wearing big thick glasses. He looked to be twelve or thirteen years old. He was sitting alone, eating lasagna. He asked if I was looking for someone, so I described you and your brother. He said he hadn't seen anyone who fit that description. We small-talked a little, then before I knew it, I was deep in serious conversation with this engaging young man. He said his name was Ronald Reagan Kim and his parents came to America from Korea in 1985, a few years before he was born. This guy must have an IQ of 200. He knew more American history than I know. He talked about physics and Einstein's theory of relativity. He talked about natural science and marine biology and astronomy, you name it. He told me that kids his age would be the first ones to make contact with extraterrestrials and that it would all take place online. So I was thinking, even though I had been stood up by some cyber-flake, it was almost worth my nearly 900 mile round trip to meet this little wizard. I was also thinking it would take a teacher to fully appreciate this precocious and brilliantly sagacious little fellow.

I insisted on paying for Ronald's lunch. He had actually gotten *you* off my mind for a while. Funny, a kid that age, eating lasagna all by himself at a restaurant on a Saturday. Such a grown-up boy, I thought.

As we walked out of Mama Mia's together, I looked at my watch and it was 1:15, Nashville time. I thought I'd go back inside and wait another fifteen minues before heading back for Tifton. I bade Ronald goodbye, and he quickly crossed the street, heading toward some apartment complexes. I was still standing at the restaurant door when he turned around to me and yelled, "AGPROF! GLAM-NASH!" then turned and ran as fast as he could. I stood there puzzled for a few seconds before I realized I had never shared our screen names with him. Then it hit me all at once.

"You little *asshole*," I screamed. For just a second I wanted to break your neck, Mr. Ronald "Glamnash," but of course I wouldn't lay a finger on a kid. I was plenty ticked off, though. I was still fuming as I pulled onto I-24 a few minutes later. By the time I was halfway to Chattanooga, I was smiling. As I crossed the Georgia state line, I was laughing hysterically.

That was pretty smart of you, assuming that a Georgia boy might well have been raised a Southern Baptist and, being a history professor, maybe I wasn't as apt to be a regular churchgoer. And you thought "independent" might not be too far off for my politics, Georgia now being heavily Republican but again, I'm a college pro-fessor, so maybe I'm a tad more liberal than the average Georgian. Yes, you had me thinking that Glamnash and I had *everything* in common. And that crap about Alan Jackson's swimming pool. Ha. You little jerk. And I was all excited about this *mature* version of Britney Spears.

I've heard that a lot of these urban legends are started by pubescent computer nerds like you. If you can make an underpaid history teacher take a 900 mile round trip to see someone he met online who claims she looks like Britney Spears, then just think what you can do someday to ease pain and suffering in the world, to say nothing of getting us off on the right foot with creatures from outer space.

Good joke, good luck

Agprof

P.S. As soon as I send you this e-mail, I'm changing my screen name.

>━━

Bobby Braddock

In a career spanning four decades, Bobby Braddock has left his mark in almost every facet of the country music industry. Having grown up in rural Central Florida during the latter days of the Jim Crow era, he began his Nashville years in the road band of the late-great Marty Robbins. From the mid-1960s to the early 1980s, Braddock was a recording artist for five major labels, but it was as a songwriter that he would enjoy quick and continuing success.

His string of thirteen number-one songs (thirty-three in the top ten) includes such classics as Tammy Wynette's "D-I-V-O-R-C-E" in 1968 and George Jones's "He

Stopped Loving Her Today" in 1980, both of which he wrote with his friend and mentor Curly Putman, as well as the Jones-Wynette duet "Golden Ring," which he wrote with Rafe Van Hoy. Bobby's hit streak continued through the 1990s as a solo writer with smashes like "Time Marches On" and "Texas Tornado."

Inducted into the Nashville Songwriters Hall of Fame in 1981, he is the two-time winner (five-time nominee) of the CMA Song of the Year Award, and has received various other accolades, including Grammy nominations. In 2001, he wrote one of the biggest hits of the new millennium, a major crossover and country's only number-one rap song, "I Wanna Talk About Me," made famous by superstar Toby Keith.

As a producer, he worked with Blake Shelton with great success—the ultimate result of this collaboration was three albums with sales totaling in the millions, and twelve weeks at the top of the country singles charts.

His memoir Down in Orburndale: A Songwriter's Youth in Old Florida, cowritten by Michael Kosser, was published by Louisiana State University Press in spring 2007.

Gathering Together

Robert Hicks

I was eight when I wandered into my grandmother's living room and met up, for the first time, with my great-uncle Willis Phinnaeus Buford, over on the sofa. Though I had never actually seen him before, he needed no introduction.

I panicked. There before me was the bane of my family.

My brothers and cousins and I had been painfully aware of Uncle Willis's presence at all family gatherings, as far back as any of us could remember. Yet, while the older ones often claimed to have seen him, I don't believe that any really had—before I encountered him there on my grandmother's sofa. My great-aunt Willie never went anywhere without him, but was not one to parade him around like the freak he had become. When we dared ask our parents why Aunt Willie never let us see him, our parents told us, "She cares too much to have y'all gawking at him and asking uncomfortable questions"—as if such an answer could be enough.

And so he remained the unseen visitor at every gathering: a presence never addressed or spoken of, except in whispers, when Willis and Willie were out of earshot.

To my grandmother, Mattie Louise Talmadge Fort, both Aunt Willie and Uncle Willis were black marks against—and embarrassments to—our clan. Only blood—our family's and Jesus'—made their presence in the least bit tolerable.

My grandmother considered many things to be black marks against our family: for instance, she didn't care for us to be in any way linked to the more famous Talmadge family of Georgia politics. They, too, were a black mark on our good name. If someone asked her if we were kin, she would smile the smile of Southern women and say, "Now do we really look like Georgians?" as if somehow Georgians looked different from those who hailed from west Tennessee. In truth, she could have cared less that those Talmadges were from Georgia; it was that they were the worst kind of politicians—those who scared poor ignorant white folks into voting for them by talking about the "Colored Threat."

Our own brand of racism, like everything else in our family, was far gentler and had grown softer with age. We were secure in our position in this world, and loved "our people" as *our* people. My grandmother loved the colored families that surrounded her and made her life click along smoothly in its place; she probably loved them more than she loved her white family. She prayed for them, fervently. She longed to be in their company in this life, and looked forward to being with them for eternity in the next.

Grandmother was far more confident that she would be spending eternity surrounded by those she loved than she was with the knowledge that her young sister, my Aunt Willie, and her husband, my Uncle Willis, would be with her.

Aunt Willie was weak. She was timid, helpless, and made poor choices in life. I knew all this by the time I was eight. Southern women *act* weak—they always have. They're supposed to act weak. But acting is never to be confused with being. It's all part of their role. While they acted, they sent their husbands and sons to war, ran the farms and stores, kept their families together, nursed their children and their people's children and their wounded when it all went bad. They were the ones who buried their dead, who fought off the invaders, who put life back together afterwards. They were the ones who kept the sacred memory of the heroic past. And they did it all without ever giving up the act.

Willie was different from the very start, if I was to believe my Aunt Mary-Charles (named after their father, my great-grandfather, Charles Philip Talmadge, "most recently of the Confederacy," whatever that meant, seeing as the war had been over almost a hundred years).

Willie never fit in. When her sisters were courting a houseful of boys who showed up in the last years of the nineteenth century, Willie was in her room, not really doing very much of anything as she waited for everyone to clear out. In fairness, Willie was not considered a beauty, as the rest of the Talmadge girls were renowned to be: She was painfully plain. While her sisters helped their mother and their grandmothers, took classes, played tennis and rode, Willie never did. She was not a reader or a cook or a helper. She seemed doomed to become that sister every family had: who never married, but stayed at home to care for her aging parents. But in Willie's case, her aging parents and her sisters and the help took care of *her*.

When her parents finally passed, her sister and brother-in-law—my grandmother and grandfather—provided her an apartment within their rambling Colonial Revival pile. My grandfather, though self-made and a product of the New South's industrial rebirth, was quick to adopt the ways of the Old South. My grandmother, a Talmadge of Talmadgeville, Tennessee, was key. She was twenty-something years his junior and lovely, the product of generation after generation of good alliances and beautiful young wives. By all accounts, they were devoted to each other.

This was their lives: gentle, gracious, uneventful; lives built around the Methodist-Episcopal Church–South, the Colonial Dames, the DAR, the UDC, bridge games, horses, dogs, garden clubs, the cotton crop, books, travel, antiquing, gossip, and my grandmother's grandchildren.

And into that world came Willis Phinnaeus Buford. He would prove to be a thirty-seven-year disruption of their carefully scripted way of life.

Willie met him in the lobby of the Peabody Hotel in Memphis. That is all any of us were ever told. Within days, though he was near twenty years younger and far handsomer than she, they were married in a civil ceremony in Stuttgart, Arkansas.

Even she had no idea about his past, his people, or his place. He cut off anyone who dared inquire—by saying he found such conversation shallow and meaningless. Meaningless? Who your people were was the bedrock of our civilization. Were we anything more than our past? My grandmother had leather-bound volumes, embossed in genuine gold, that told our story, taking the "Talmadge and Allied Families" back to 1066, and linking us to all the important events of history (even if we had to skip a generation or two, now and then, to get us there).

Once Willie and Willis had settled into one of my grandfather's many comfortable non-rented rental houses populated by my grandmother's family, Willis seemed to find work as shallow and meaningless as any discussion of his past. Though he was, according to his wife, always "on the threshold of something very big," Willis never seemed to make it through the door and into the temple of success.

All his schemes and travel, like everything else, were

financed by his wife, who was, if truth be known, financed by my grandfather; and when he passed, by my grandmother.

That was all we knew. Willis seemed to have no hobbies, no friends, and few interests, including his wife.

For thirty-seven years, Willis Phinnaeus Buford mooched off our family, stayed away for months at a time, and made my great-aunt seem even more pathetic while she longed for his returns and lived her life in his vacuum. By all reports, even when he was around, he wasn't. He had found a meal ticket with few demands.

And then one day in 1948, three years before I was born, the phone rang. Uncle Willis had passed. He had been found dead in a hotel room in Greenwood, Mississippi, by a lady who worked as a salesclerk at a local department store. His heart.

I have few doubts that my grandmother rested far easier that evening knowing we were rid, once and for all, of ol' Willis. Just as my aunt began to veil herself in mourning, as far as my grandmother was concerned, a far bigger veil had been lifted from our family and its good name. While I'm sure they took on their prescribed roles as comforters to their grieving sister, as far as the rest of the Talmadge "girls" were concerned, relief and justice had finally arrived for the righteous.

My grandmother set about making the arrangements for his interment in one of the seventy-one remaining spaces in the Talmadge-Fort plot in the center of Rest Haven Cemetery on the highest spot in Madison County, just outside the edge of Talmadgeville.

And then they read his will. Willis Phinnaeus Buford did not want to wait out the long sleep before Judgment Day with our clan. He was to be cremated, and his ashes spread from a boat in the dead center of the Mississippi, between Tennessee and

Arkansas. He was very clear that a bridge would not do. He wanted to be launched from a boat.

No one in our family had ever been cremated. Cremation was a dark ritual of the Pagans in some far-off woods. The only time you could possibly allow a Methodist to be cremated was if he had died in a terrible fire and you were simply finishing the job. When Willis died, our people still held to the belief that an open coffin provided comfort for loved ones. For some unknown reason, the living found comfort in seeing that the dead were really dead. The same photographer who photographed our weddings would drive from Memphis out to Talmadgeville to photograph our dead: in case an "out-of-towner" had to miss the funeral, all the good food, and the chance to see a loved one dead, face to face, one last time. Folks would "talk" if you didn't have a proper, open coffin or there wasn't any cold fried chicken afterward.

If it had been any real member of our family or any other in-law, my grandmother would have ignored the cremation request. She would have reminded, gently, those who mourned that such a request was made by someone not in his or her right mind. "What if he had asked to be stuffed and mounted? Would we follow his wishes and drive on over to the taxidermist?" Her arguments would have been clear and overwhelming. We *buried* our dead.

But Uncle Willis was not a real member of our family, nor was he any other in-law. Willis was a worthless leech and a black mark and didn't deserve one of our seventy-one remaining spaces. My grandmother was just being gracious to her pitiful sister even to have offered. He would have to fend for himself on Judgment Day when the quick and the dead rose up at the sound of the last trumpet and all the rest of us were together.

So Willis Buford was cremated as he had wished, and life went on filled with church and bridge, travels and grandchildren.

Except for one small hiccup.

When they gave Aunt Willie the small green box with reinforced metal corners that contained Willis, she never seemed able to get around to renting the boat and following the second half of his wishes.

No matter how much coercion—ever so gentle at first, then not so gentle at all—the family placed on her, Willie seemed finally to have what she never had in his life: Willis, one hundred percent of him.

Whether she always carried him around in her purse or if that only came in time, I don't know. But by the time my brothers and cousins and I came along, all of us knew that Uncle Willis stayed in Aunt Willie's handbag.

For several years after his death, he remained in the green box. Eventually the box, having been designed as a temporary home, began to leak at the seams, so Willie, still resisting her sisters' well-founded logic, transferred Willis to a glass quart canning jar with an orange rubber ring-seal. And then he went back in her purse.

Though none of our generation ever really knew Willis Buford, all of us knew that purse and all the other purses that followed over the years. None of us ever entered a room and weren't immediately aware of the location of Uncle Willis.

As much as Uncle Willis was a very real part of my childhood and our family visits back to Talmadgeville and my grandmother's farm, there is something not right, even in our family, about a woman who carried her dead husband around with her in a Mason jar.

No one else I knew had any of their relatives in jars. Why our family? And while it seemed to fit, with all the rest... my family living in the atomic age of the 1950s but still making references to the Civil War's effects on us, it just didn't seem right.

And so that November day, just a few days before Thanksgiving 1959, I finally saw Uncle Willis, his jar leaning back on a pillow on my grandmother's sofa, taken out of his dark leather tomb by my great-aunt for some reason I will never know. My brothers didn't believe me when I said I had finally seen him. Their adamant disbelief seemed to confirm my belief that I was, indeed, the first of us to see him.

We had all come home, as we had every year, a family joined together—not that we ever were too long away, no matter where we lived. All of my grandmother's sisters were still well and thriving, and, as they had all their lives, were still preparing the dinner.

Thanksgiving was the one day in the year when Minnie, my grandmother's beloved cook and best friend, was pushed aside and became simply a lackey in the kitchen where she proudly ruled.

Every year, the old place came back to life—it was a glimpse of how it must have been when my dad was growing up. As each of the sisters prepared her "dish," the doors to the back hall and to the dining room swung back and forth as old servants were sent on missions to get this and do that. There was a commotion that was rarely found in a house now populated with old folks.

Willie didn't really have a dish. She got in folks' way. No one really needed her help, but part of everyone's job was to try to find small jobs she could do, here and there.

And then everything began to go wrong. As best as we could later piece together, Willie pulled Willis out of her purse and set him on the mantel. With everyone working and talking and ordering folks around, no one noticed that Willis had been placed right there in the midst of it all.

Great-aunt Tump, the godliest of all, was making her mother's mother's signature cornbread dressing—as she had since her mother had given over the reins forty years before. This was no ordinary cornbread dressing from a package. This was holy, sacred dressing, far more important and more at the center of our meal than any turkey would ever claim. This was the dressing whose recipe all our mothers had asked for, in preparation for the day Tump left us.

Tump was looking for black pepper. There had never been the need for her to bother others. She could find it herself. Why interrupt a good story just to ask for the pepper?

She found, up on the mantel, a quart jar of black pepper.

Before she began to spoon and stir Uncle Willis into the dressing, she tasted him. Tump would go to her grave with her cherished faith that he was black pepper—that the crematorium must have given him a good Christian burial and then dumped a large can of black pepper into Willis's green box. After all, the crematorium people knew as well as anyone that they shouldn't be burning folks up. Aunt Tump would remain alone with this belief.

Aunt Willie must have noticed the opening of a too-familiar jar: she collapsed, swooning, onto the linoleum. Everything stopped. She was out cold, but seemed still to be with us.

My grandmother's equally elderly physician, Dr. Crook, came from his farm next door, arriving after Willie had been taken to her bed. As she came to, she mumbled things that made no sense: but then, again, when had she ever made much sense?

Somehow her sisters pieced it all together. Tump was mortified. Her actions had, all at the same time, hurt her fragile sister and ruined the dressing. My grandmother, meanwhile, was not going to throw away a very large pan of cornbread dressing just because of a small mistake. After all, she had lived through the Great Depression, when folks would have killed for a very large pan of cornbread dressing—and such cornbread dressing as this!

On the other hand, no one seemed too concerned about Willis. After some quiet discussion, Grandmother decided to get Willis out of the dressing and back in his jar. Of course it was understood that, even when she'd finished, there was bound to be some dressing in the jar and Willis in the dressing. Nothing was perfect in this life, but we could try our best. That's all He had ever asked of us.

The kitchen oath was the key to making it through the day. My grandmother made each of her sisters, including a sniveling Aunt Tump and all the servants, swear they would never tell another soul what had happened. Willie had simply taken to her bed, as she more than anyone else would do. Success rested on their silence. What had happened was no one's business. It was over, done.

By the time we gathered in the dining room that afternoon, the big table a bit bigger and the four "children's" tables filled in each corner, everyone knew. I'd heard it from my cousin Pat.

It was a rather quiet Thanksgiving. None of the grandchildren needed to be reminded that we were inside a house, or at dinner. There were no outbursts as we all kept our eyes glued on what seemed to be an unusually large serving of dressing on each of our plates. It looked, in fact, like most everything on our plates was dressing, the rest of the meal a mere garnish. Each of us had the same goal, and that was to make it through the meal and try not to eat anything that had touched the dressing.

My grandmother tried to normalize the unusually quiet meal with small talk. She demanded verbal interaction. Yet silence seemed to prevail, broken only by the periodic quiet sniveling of Aunt Tump.

As I said earlier, weakness was never considered a virtue in our family. When significant looks didn't work, Grandmother spoke up and asked Tump why she was sniffing and dabbing at her eyes. She knew perfectly well why, of course; what she was really saying, in her own special way, was to stop.

Tump, by now so eaten up with grief and guilt, didn't take the hint. "You perfectly well know why!"

Grandmother again tried to take control. "No. I don't understand why."

This was Tump's cue to silence, but somehow she didn't get it. "I'm sniveling because Willis is in the dressing and Willie's in her bed! That's why I'm sniveling! It's all wrong and you know it!"

It was out. What we all already knew was now public knowledge. Willis was in the dressing. Willie really did have a reason this time to have taken to her bed. Despite Tump's weeping, our silence grew louder.

And then it happened. All of us are witness to what was said and happened next. Our grandmother cut that silence with a slight smile and melodious words. "No, I don't understand why you're sniveling. Here we are, an unbroken chain of family under one roof. The Lord has preserved our health and made us to prosper. We are united as sisters in this family, with my children and my children's children. Our land and our people thrive and are well. We are safe here from harm's way.

"It was bad enough that Willis Buford ever came into our lives. He humiliated our vulnerable sister with his slothfulness and infidelity. It was bad enough that he died as he did, compromising what was left of her dignity. It was bad enough that he demanded to be cremated as heathens do and thrown into the Mississippi—for what purpose I will never understand. Yet even then she could not depart from him and has humiliated each of us by carrying him around in a jar for near fifteen years.

"I'm not sure that Willis Buford didn't finally do something constructive for this family that he only took from in life."

"Whatever could you mean?" Tump asked.

And then we saw her do it. For the first time that anyone could recall, my grandmother, Mattie Louise Talmadge Fort, with her impeccable table manners, took a bite of food *and spoke with her mouth full*. "If I'm not mistaken," she said as she shifted the food on her palate, "I believe that Willis has added a bit of body to the dressing."

And with that, all the taboos had disappeared, the veil had lifted. At first with reluctance, and then with some kind of empowerment years before any of us had ever heard the word, each of us, in our own time and in our own way, ate Uncle Willis.

Within the next two years my grandmother and the rest of the Talmadge "girls" went on to their reward. All who gathered with them around the big table that day are now gone, too. There are far fewer spaces left in the Talmadge-Fort lot at Rest Haven these days.

Yet, for those of us who remain, Willis Buford forever lives on in our hearts every year, as we gather together, wherever we might be.

Robert Hicks

Robert Hicks has lived and worked in Nashville for over thirty years. As a music publisher, he has run his own company, launching the careers of some of Nashville's best-loved singer-songwriters. He has worked as an independent publisher and has also been in partnerships with both PolyGram Music and MCA/Universal Music.

His regular "guitar pulls" out at his cabin in the hills south of Nashville have attracted everyone from Mary Chapin Carpenter and the late Harlan Howard to John Hiatt and Tom T. Hall; from Jules Shear and Larry Carlton to Ray Wylie Hubbard and Steppenwolf's John Kay. Keith Richards once remarked, "You just don't stumble upon the guitar pull, you have to persevere in your heart to get there."

As a writer, his essays on regional history, Southern material culture, furniture, and music have appeared in numerous publications over the years. His first book, a collaboration with French-American photographer Michel Arnaud, came out in 2000: Nashville: The Pilgrims of Guitar Town *(Stewart, Tabori & Chang).*

His debut novel, The Widow of the South *(Warner Books, New York, 2005), was born out of his many years of work at Historic Carnton Plantation in Franklin, Tennessee, and his passion for the preservation of the remaining fragments of the battlefield.* The Widow of the South *was launched to overwhelming critical success and became a* New York Times *Best Seller. In December 2005, Hicks was named Tennessean of the Year by the* Nashville Tennessean *for the impact* The Widow of the South *has had on Tennessee. He is currently at work on his next novel.*

The Point

Monty Powell

Which one is it, Daddy?" asked ten-year-old Carolina.
"I'm not sure," came the reply from the other side of the SUV. "It's hard to tell—none of these houses used to be here."

Richard Nance was telling the truth. When he and his family had made their annual pilgrimages to Fripp Island, South Carolina, in the early 1970s, none of this long row of ostentatious beachfront retreats had been built, save one, which still existed a world apart from the rest. It was perched on the last gasping point of this tiny three-and-a-half-mile-long barrier island, commanding a view of the ever-changing sandbars that loosely defined the southernmost tip of its domain. The house was a lone sentinel, the last outpost, as ahead of the curve of the 1970s Southern real estate renaissance as Da Vinci was ahead of his own in fifteenth-century Italy.

Every summer since the late sixties, Richard's family had rented this same retreat precisely because it was so isolated. For a mile on either side of the house there had stretched only unbroken sand, sea oats, and slate gray water. Gulls and sandpipers had outnumbered sunbathers a thousand to one. Back then, the pavement simply ended as the last, long thrust of this isolated spit pointed its finger, like Adam, into the watery Sistine Chapel of the Atlantic, stretching its way to the God of the mainland. Physically, the land was close enough almost to touch across a ribbon of tidal creek that could be waded in less-than-knee-deep water on the right low tide, but psychologically, it was an insurmountable geographical feature that would always separate the islanders from their landlocked neighbors.

To Richard Nance and his family, that last mile where civilization ended and the road became two beckoning concave tracks in the sand was the most holy ground on the planet. To bump across the last blacktop speed bump and onto that seldom-traveled lane signaled freedom. Freedom from school and work, freedom from the dog-day swelter and humidity that covered north Georgia every summer as completely as the wall-to-wall carpeting made in its ramshackle mills covered sumptuous living rooms from New York to San Diego.

It signaled the start of the week that everyone dreamed about all year long. So powerful was the pull of this hallowed place and this sacred time that Richard's hyper-extended family—including aunts, great-uncles, and twice- or even thrice-removed cousins—would begin packing months in advance. Meticulous grocery lists were drawn up and haggled over. A sumptuous menu was created and teams of people from different families were assigned a respective night of the week to carefully prepare their specialty: roast beef or "Fripp meat," as it was so casually called, Melea's spaghetti, Mama Joy's chocolate chip cake. Everyone had their thoroughbred dish, and each one would get its chance to run. For one week out of the hectic year the whole extended family simply packed up and moved. They traded their tiny north Georgia hamlet of Resaca, so claustrophobically hemmed in by I-75 on one side and old Highway 41 on the other, for a paradise bounded only by the endless salt marshes to the rear and the limitless horizon of the unending ocean to the front.

"I think this is the one, honey," Richard said as he picked Carolina up and placed her bare feet on the too-hot hood of his Ford Explorer.

"Ouch, Daddy!" she cried.

"Sorry, baby," he said as he placed her down in the even hotter sand.

"Daddy," she protested. So he swept her up in his arms and held her there, trying to get his bearings, letting the years peel away until he could picture this place thirty-five years ago and hopefully spot the reason he had made this detour in the first place.

"Yes," he said softly, "that has to be it."

Old and battered, the house kneeled in the shadow of the magnificent mansionettes that had been erected on either side of it. He laughed to himself as he eyed the clumsy new structures. Rambling, overwrought, and architecturally vapid were his immediate thoughts. It was as if some rich Atlanta socialite had eaten an entire mall of Restoration Hardware stores and then vomited on a series of empty waterfront lots. He laughed as he thought of how they had purchased their nostalgia, and a curious sense of pride welled up in him at the thought of the many years it took to earn his.

For years the lone house that was now so besieged had been the roof over as many as twenty people at a time for the big week. There were pallets and couches, air mattresses and sleeping bags scattered around upstairs. Kids slept at the feet of the beds of their parents, boyfriends and unacknowledged lovers were relegated to the dank basement, where palmetto bugs and

mosquitoes fought for dominion over the crowded little bed-
rooms that housed the transient vacationers. Who was to say
if the same boyfriend would be around next year? For decades
the basement held a parade of ever-changing temporary family
members who, for a week at least, were considered Nances and
treated like part of the family.

The house was, as often seems to be the case, smaller
than he remembered. In his mind as a child it had towered
over the point like a striding medieval castle. Now it looked
plain squatty. Its old-school Florida cinder-block basement and
peeling cedar siding looked cheap and insubstantial next to
the fifteen-foot cement pilings and Masonite clapboard of its
upscale neighbors. But, no doubt, this was it; this was where
he'd grown up. At least that's how he had always seen it: as a
kid he had lived fifty-one weeks of his life in the gentle foot-
hills of the worn-down Blue Ridge Mountains, but for reasons
still unknown to him, he had always marked his passage time
here. Everyone else's years ran from either January to January
or from birthday to birthday, but not for him—no, in his mind
he would always grow up here, summer to summer.

"Can we go inside, Daddy?" Carolina asked.

"No, honey, we can't," he said. "But let's walk around it
a bit."

He held her hand as they picked their way through the
sea oats and sand spurs to a well-worn path that led through
a rickety gate to the front of the house. The sight of the old
screened porch, still jutting out majestically over the dunes,
dilapidated but stately, the queen of the point, wearing the
rouge of thousands of blustery saltwater days and the patina of
too many slanting setting suns, brought an upwelling of something untouched in him for a long time. Richer than nostalgia and purer than melancholy, it was like a vortex, the null

point where joy and pain cancel each other out and you are left wholly with your own accounting of just how much of yourself you can bequeath to one place, to one experience. For Richard, it was like finding a pocket full of twenties in an old pair of jeans, but every bill had his picture on it and the currency was his very life.

He had told Carolina the stories so many times that she knew the punch lines by heart, but standing here flicking the sugary white sand up with their toes, he felt it become real for her for the first time. He was introducing her to a long-lost friend, like a pen pal she'd known so well from a distance then finally got to embrace. This house, his family, his story. She got it; he could tell. And that was enough.

As they rounded the other side of the fence on their way out, he noticed that a police car with a flashing light had pulled in behind his parked Explorer. As he got closer he saw it wasn't a cop car at all, but a sedan labeled FRIPP ISLAND SECURITY.

"This your Explorer?" the fake cop asked.

"Yes it is. Is there a problem...er...Officer?" Richard asked, trying not to show contempt for the guy, whose only job was to make sure "undesirable" people didn't loiter too long around real estate they clearly couldn't afford.

"No problem," he said, "just saw you had a visitor's pass for the day and you really can't park here unless you own or are renting property."

"I used to own a lot here," Richard said, which was true. Years ago, in a different marriage and what now seemed like a whole other life, he had taken what savings he had and purchased a tiny interior lot on the small trickle of a tidal creek that poured in and out twice daily through the bowels of the island. That this qualified as "waterfront" was still something of a great inside joke to him, but, like every other piece of dry sand within a five iron of the ocean, it had increased in value at a rate far quicker than any other investment he had ever made. It had been sold as part of the amicable but gut-wrenching divorce settlement between himself and Carolina's mom. At the time, so much in his life was questioned and unanswered that he hadn't cared. Now he suddenly felt like he had pawned his childhood dream and couldn't get it back.

He stood there in the uncomfortable silence between him and the "officer" and chewed on the disorienting feeling of being considered an outsider.

He glanced down at Carolina and watched her as she carefully placed a tiny sun-bleached, skull-white scallop shell she had found deep into her pocket. He silently wondered how many million children before her and before him had absently walked along some long-forgotten sandy trail and innocently reached down to harvest some tidbit that caught their eye. He marveled over how uniquely human it was to try to capture in a solid sculpted form the wonder and timelessness of a moment written only in wind and tide and memory. She had found a shell that was forever to be her token of this long-awaited encounter with his past.

He knew instinctively that they would never speak about it, that she would cherish it always and that it would reside in some special, out-of-the-way place in the homes she would make as she grew into a woman. It seemed such a small and insignificant gesture, but with it his mind was suddenly and forcefully knocked down like a child hit by a rogue wave. He felt like he was being swept along by the riptide current of time, slowly sinking into the full realization that for most of his natural life, his immovable intention had been to raise a family, make his mark in the business world, and then to retire here. He was to come full circle back to the place that had defined his youth and make his final rite of passage here at the confluence of this sand and water, to grow, and to grow old, embracing his death like a lover, to let the full experience of it rush through him like the wonder and awe of a first kiss on a sunset pier and to let the ocean be the only witness to the seduction powers of the last great mystery, the last great mistress. He had counted his years here. He could trace every significant milestone event in his younger life back to this spot. Surely, he thought, this is where it would also end.

He knew now in an instant that it was not to be. The island and its lifelong hold on him would fade after this trip. New memories would rush in like the eight-foot floods that daily blanketed the saw grass and mudflats. The aching pull of those glorious summers would slip away as silently as the redfish tails on an autumn ebb tide.

Carolina looked up at him and said, "Daddy, thanks for showing me where you grew up." Her small voice broke the spell.

Richard laughed easily. "You're welcome, sweetheart." He winked at her. "You were named for this state, you know."

"I know, Dad—you've told me a hundred times," she said.

He looked over at the security guard, who had that twitchy look in his eye of a voyeur who has seen something too secret and sacred. "Officer, we'll be leaving now," he said.

The man slowly tipped his hat, nervously shuffled back over to his car, and eased away.

Richard cranked the Explorer and felt the compressor struggle to cool them off as he sat there for a moment idling. Carolina was quiet, looking out the window and silently toying with the newfound souvenir in her pocket. He slipped the car into Drive and slowly rolled away.

Although the pavement was smooth before him, in his soul

he felt the jostling of the deeply worn ruts from so many years ago. He had shared his most vulnerable self with his own flesh and blood, and he had learned more than he had taught. He knew now he would not die here and that he would not return again to this spot in this life. But he also knew with the unerring certainty that only comes when fathers are alone with their daughters that when it was his turn to die, and he lay in rest, that a small, white scallop shell would find its way into his folded hands. He would make the final journey over sand and sea to the island of the last secret keeper, where he would rejoin the boy he was at ten and twelve and sixteen and the man at twenty-one and thirty. He would embrace these separated souls of himself, the memories that had spoken to him so often and had waited so patiently for his return in an eternal dance as fluid and powerful as the cresting waves of his childhood.

She would remember. She would do that for him.

Monty Powell

As a music-business veteran for nearly twenty-five years, Resaca, Georgia, native Monty Powell has successfully honed his craft and found his niche as a songwriter-producer who often collaborates with such artists as Keith Urban, Chris Cagle, Rascal Flatts, James Otto, Diamond Rio, and many more. His recent successes like the multi-week number-one singles "Days Go By" and "Tonight I Wanna Cry" for Keith Urban, and "Miss Me Baby" and top-five hit "What a Beautiful Day" for Chris Cagle keep him at the forefront of Nashville's top tunesmiths.

Apart from songwriting, Powell coproduced Diamond Rio's first three albums, two of which are now platinum and one gold. In 1994, he won a CMA Album of the Year Award for his production work on Common Thread: The Songs of the Eagles. In addition, Powell produced "Working Man's Blues" by Jed Zepplin (Steve Wariner, Lee Roy Parnell, and Diamond Rio) on the highly acclaimed Mamma's Hungry Eyes: A Tribute to Merle Haggard. Powell also produced and engineered jazz-pop singer-songwriter Anna Wilson's debut record, The Long Way (Asylum / Curb), and her sophomore effort, Time Changes (2007).

Monty currently writes for Universal Music Publishing Group, and has recently written songs that will soon be released on upcoming albums for Rascal Flatts, James Otto, Aaron Lines, and Anna Wilson, among others.

Monty resides in Nashville when he is not chasing fish with a fly rod on the gulf coast of Florida. You can visit his Web site at www.montypowell.com.

Mr. Munch Has a Murmur

Mark D. Sanders

I can only write in the first person; it's the only person I can write in. I me me, I me me, I me me I. "It's always all about you"—that's how my ex likes to put it, and she likes to put it right between the eyes: kapow, knock me down, bruise my ego, beat the crap out of me in a very civilized way. And I used to take it hard, but now I hardly take the time to listen. And even if I did listen it'd still be the first person for me. Always. But lucky for us she plays no part in this story and we don't have to worry about her busting in with a helping of her righteous indignation, which is the only indignation of which she is capable. Forget that shit. Leave it in the past.

The past, that's when this happens, but I can't tell you exactly when 'cause right now I don't know for sure exactly what, and anyway you tell me who ever knows for sure what happened, ever. And when did you show up here, and how do you know you're somebody I want to read this. You don't know my ex, do you? God forbid you tell her and she calls or writes one of those letters, and I see it's her and know if I open the envelope or pick up the phone there will be a price for my soul to pay. If you're a friend of hers please stop reading right this minute, stop reading and go get yourself one of those chocolate croissants. Share it with her other friend.

So I was in New York, a place I've only been to twice, being from and loyal to the West and wanting to travel in that direction when I travel. But I was in New York this time, because I had to be because that's where the story happens. And there are sidewalks in New York and on the sidewalks are people walking, lots of people walking, and people selling hot dogs and sugar-coated peanuts, which will make you a little sick if you eat two bags in a row. Yes and there are people with briefcases full of watches and people with bedspreads and blankets full of knockoff purses and those people are moving most of the time only a few steps ahead of those who are Policemen. Oh—and there are the people who are homeless except for this particular sidewalk and maybe that particular set of stairs down to the subway when the subway doors are locked and available for leaning.

I am walking. The sidewalk is crowded so I reach back to make sure my wallet is there. My wallet is there, so I reach down to make sure my zipper is zipped. My zipper is zipped so I rub my nose to make sure there isn't something hanging off my nose, something that might offend even a New Yorker who must not be too easily offended if the sidewalks are like this all the time, but something that would offend my ex because of her refined sensibilities, way more refined than mine ever were since I was from the West and my family was in no way sophisticated or cultured or mannerly and she was from the South where they still like a little class distinction and where you can tell which families are hanging in there with a bit of success because they're in church on Sunday. No, not the new suburban nondenominational church but the Methodist and Episcopal and Baptist and of course the Presbyterian, where the bankers wear the same suits they wear to work, or at mass on Saturday night, something I still don't understand, why Catholics want to do what they do on Saturday night at 5:30. But she kept telling her parents that it—our getting maried—would work out. It didn't and there wasn't, not in my nose at least.

Something needs to happen, and soon, or I'm gonna lose you. Or are you gonna be like my ex and keep threatening to leave but never go 'cause where the hell was she gonna go, who would have her, you tell me. But come what may my phone rings, right there on the sidewalk:

"Mr. Sanders, this is Elizabeth at Dr. Fawcett's office. I'm sorry, but can you hold a moment, please?"

You go to New York, you gotta do something with the cat, so you leave him at the vet's and you figure why not get his oil checked while he's there so you tell the vet yeah, check him out, see if he's a quart low smile smile smile. And the next thing you know you're standing on the sidewalk, stopping traffic, on hold. Mamma Mia, Thoroughly Modern Millie, Toys "R" Us, these are the thoughts running through my mind as I wait for his majesty the doggie doctor. And who would name a cat Munchkin and call him Mr. Munch, which means, as a former friend likes to point out, that I got a pussy named Mr. Munch. Who needs friends, anyway.

"Mr. Sanders, are you still there?"

"Oh yes, I am Mr. Sanders and I am still here."

"Thank you so much for holding, Mr. Sanders," she says, and I'm thinking who's holding Mr. Sanders, nobody, that's who, and, "Oh Mr. Sanders, I'm so sorry to disturb you on your trip but something is terribly wrong with Mr. Munch!"

"Something is so wrong with my little cat," I say sheepishly, trying to maintain the animal theme, "that you have called me here on the sidewalks of New York?"

"Oh yes, Mr. Sanders, Dr. Fawcett just now finished Mr. Munch's checkup, and I have his notes right here in my hand."

"And?" And then a pregnant pause.

"Mr. Munch has a murmur!"

(Would that the vet were giving my ex a checkup, they could call and say, "Mr. Sanders we fear the bitch has a murmur," which words would be within the approved vocabulary for these folks, and I could say, "Oh, don't worry about it, just put her back in the kennel, which rhymes with fennel." But she's talking about my cat, the one with the long white hair and the cute name and pretty eyes.)

And the cop is saying, "Move along," to the sellers of various counterfeit items and to the homeless and to me, the guy with the cat with the murmur.

"Elizabeth, are your sure this is my Munch he examined? And since when did cats start having heart murmurs?"

"Oh yes, I'm afraid it is, Mr. Sanders. And cats are not unlike any other animals with hearts (they don't know my ex). There can be problems. But let me tell you what our options are here."

"Yeah," I tell the cop, "I'm moving, I'm moving all right."

"Yeah," I tell Elizabeth. "What are the options?" (Knowing I have no pussy health insurance, no deductible, no co-pay, no money.)

"Well, first off we probably need to do an ultrasound, not unlike the ultrasound they perform on pregnant women."

(When my ex was pregnant I wasn't looking for the baby's heartbeat—I was looking for my ex's, wondering was there one in there somewhere.)

"There's a fine vet in town who'll do that for you, and then we can decide on the course of treatment..."

(Yeah, I'm gonna need treatment by the time this is over, when the cat dies and I have a whole bottle of pussy pain pills left and I can't resist and the doc starts getting suspicious when I call in for a refill for my dead Mr. Munch.)

"...we think will be best for Munchkin. We will need to monitor his blood for blood clots, since that could be a big problem if one were to come loose and circulate to his brain."

"Cats can have strokes, huh?"

"Yes, again not unlike us humans, Mr. Sanders. But we can deal with that when you get back, we don't want to put a crimp or a cramp or even a crampon in your vacation. Just be sure to tell whoever's at the front desk that you need to see Dr. Fawcett when you come to pick up Munchkin."

I need some time to think, but this sidewalk is like a sea of humanity and the light says Walk and even the people who don't know English seem to know what to do and we're all walking together, like friends and buddies and compatriots. But surely I'm the only one with a cat with a murmur. And as that thought sinks in (has it sunk in for you yet, that I have a cat named Mr. Munch who has a murmur in his little cat heart?), I just up and stop walking and start wondering, only I guess my *compañeros* don't know that I'm wondering and just figure I've got a mind to stand in the middle of the corner of some street and some avenue in the heart of the Big Apple, like some tourist who doesn't know his butt from his mutt. I'm wondering what if the vet's wrong, what if Munch doesn't really have a murmur, or what if he's right and Munch falls over dead before I get home and how did Elizabeth know I was here on vacation anyway? And why did they invent cell phones? Only I can't really hear myself think 'cause of the taxis honking at me since

I'm the only one standing in the street and it reminds me what that former friend, who just so happens (only in a story does somebody just so happen, huh?) to be from New York, told me always to remember when in New York if I want to live to talk about New York to my kids: "Keep walking," he said to me. "Whatever you do, keep walking." And I realize I'm in violation of his rule number one, but then he's the one who made fun of my cat.

(My ex doesn't have the nerve to make fun of my cat because she has the world's meanest cat and so is operating with limited moral wiggle room when it comes to cats, though that sure as hell doesn't stop her when it comes to me, and I'm thinking maybe I should introduce my ex-friend to my ex and he can make fun of her pussy and we'll see what you-know-who has to say about that), and now my cat, Mr. Munch, has a murmur. And the taxis are making their way around me as only New York taxis can, as if they're all greased with Vaseline and bending amidships like metered bananas with wheels, and the drivers are all cursing at me in their language of choice, which seems to be running about eighty percent not English and the twenty percent that I understand I only understand because I've heard my ex say the same things, more than once.

I'm the first person I ever had sex with. She, like you, oh gentle reader, never thought that was funny, either.

And now the next group of walkers has overtaken me, the ones who were waiting for the Walk sign while the taxis were honking and winding their way around me, and these walkers want to know where the story is headed from here. They wanna know am I gonna turn around and call the vet back and tell him I'm headed home for the ultrasound 'cause I love that cat like a child, or am I gonna keep walking until I get to some museum or some restaurant or some store that they don't have back home, 'cause if they had them back home why would I be here in the first place, and when I get to whatever I'm headed to will I try to put the cat and the murmur and the whole concept of cat mortality behind me at least for the moment and will I in fact try to live in the moment for once.

(That was something my ex was big on, living in the moment, whatever the hell that means, and lord wasn't she always harping how I worried too much about the future and worried too much about the past and why couldn't I just take it one day at a time like they do in AA only I know she'd never go to AA so how does she know that's what they do, though I remember that her dad, rest his soul, was a Mason but not the kind who lays bricks, and I know they have lots of secret shit in the Masons and maybe that's where she picked it up, like she picked up every self-help book in every bookstore we ever walked into.)

And I'm wondering, how do these fellow walkers of mine know that Mr. Munch has a murmur. So I ask them, and they say to me they say, "It's written all over your face," and I say, "Am I really that transparent?" and they say, "Yeah, we can see right through you," and I say to them, "A penny for my thoughts," and they say to me, "They ain't worth it, buddy."

They like to call you buddy in New York.

The next thing you know, because it's the next thing I'm gonna tell you, the next thing you know they're picking me up, these walkers who can read my mind, and putting me on their shoulders like those football players from the University of Alabama used to put Bear Bryant on their shoulders when they won the National Championship. They carry me to the sidewalk and they set me down on the sidewalk and the closest guy with a briefcase full of watches comes over and he hands me a watch and I try to give him twenty bucks but he says, "No, pal, I don't need your money."

Then a guy with a bedspread full of purse knockoffs comes over and hands me a purse and he won't take my money either.

And then a cop walks up and he says, "You know we lost a lot of friends on nine eleven and we want you to be a friend."

Then it's a homeless guy pushing his basketful of shopping bags over to me like I need a basketful of shopping bags and then he looks me right in the eye, which is rather unlike most of these homeless guys unless they want some money, but he looks me in the eye and he says, "Hey, buddy, ain't that your phone ringin'?"

"Yeah, I guess it is."

"Mr. Sanders, Dr. Fawcett here. I'm sorry to say we've made a wee little mistake, a feline failure to communicate, if you will. After I gave your Mr. Munch a thorough once-over—which he passed like the healthy pussy he is—I picked out a costume for him to wear to our Weekly Wednesday Highwhyin' Luau and wrote that down on his report. Well, Mr. Sanders, I'm afraid that when Elizabeth glanced at the report while speaking with you earlier she mistook Mr. Munch's muumuu for a murmur and may have, I fear, caused you to worry needlessly about your little pussy."

"Worry needlessly about my little pussy?" I say to the good doctor I say, "Jeez, you don't expect me to believe that, do you? A murmur becomes a muumuu all of a sudden and instead of my cat dying prematurely he gets fat on roasted pig and spends the afternoon watching hula dancers dance the hula? Muumuu my—"

But by this time folks are beginning to get restless, seeing's how they're most of them New Yorkers, and New Yorkers aren't apt to not get restless eventually, murmur or no murmur, and so I throw down the phone and hold up both of my hands like one of those televangelists with the gray hair poofed up who tell you God loves you and then rip your wallet right out of your shorts. The bastards. Yes, verily, I hold up my hands and I say, "Brothers and Sisters, if you were to read all the way though the Bible, all the way to the end of the mighty Book of Revelations, you would by now realize that every story has an ending, and that this story is no exception (rhymes with erection, perhaps posing a bigger problem than a little pussy) and that this one is due to end (with all due respects to my ex) right about…now." Kapow. Purina Cat Chow.

>~~

Mark D. Sanders

Mark D. Sanders came to Nashville from Southern California in 1980 and decided he'd stay. He and his wife, Cindy, have five children between them, the youngest two having recently started college.

These are the number-one songs in Mark D. Sanders's music catalog: "Runnin' Behind" (Tracy Lawrence), "Money in the Bank" (John Anderson), "Whatcha Gonna Do With a Cowboy" (Chris LeDoux and Garth Brooks), "If You've Got Love" (John Michael Montgomery), "They're Playin' Our Song" (Neal McCoy), "The Heart Is a Lonely Hunter" (Reba McEntire), "It Matters to Me" (Faith Hill), "No News" (Lonestar), "Blue Clear Sky" (George Strait), "Daddy's Money" (Ricochet), "Don't Get Me Started" (Rhett Akins), "This Ain't No Thinkin' Thing" (Trace Adkins), "Come Cryin' to Me" (Lonestar), and "I Hope You Dance" (Lee Ann Womack), cowritten with Tia Sillers.

Some of the other hits he's written: "Bobbie Ann Mason"

*(Rick Trevino), "Walkin' to Jerusalem" (Tracy Byrd),
"Heads Carolina, Tails California" (Jo Dee Messina),
"My Heart Has a History" (Paul Brandt), "I'd Rather Ride
Around With You" (Reba McEntire), "Vidalia" (Sammy
Kershaw), "The Day That She Left Tulsa" (Wade Hayes),
"Mirror, Mirror" (Diamond Rio), "That'd Be All Right"
(Alan Jackson).*

*Awards include: Writer of the Year–ASCAP, Nashville
Songwriters Association (twice),* Billboard, Music Row
magazine, American Songwriter; *four CMA Triple Play
Awards (three number-ones in a twelve-month period); 2000
CMA Song of the Year; 2001 Grammy Country Song of the
Year; ASCAP Song of the Year (1997, 2001).*

Fork

John Hadley

Maybe it happened when my dad lifted me up and held me, leaning forward so I could see my grandfather. Black suit, white shirt buttoned at the neck, eyes closed, his bald head resting on a shiny pillow. So still. So quiet. The room barely breathing. Maybe then...

My grandfather, J. P. Fellers, owned and operated the sawmill down the street and around the corner from the two-story house he built in Napoleon, Ohio. A lumberman in his early seventies, six-foot-two and strong as a log chain, he smelled like sawdust. He'd sit in his rocking chair in the narrow room between the kitchen and the living room, his huge hands and open arms herding my sister and me up into his lap, hugging and tickling us, then making a big show of removing his dentures and chewing on our ears with his toothless gums, growling as we giggled. My sister was seven, I was four. We loved Grampa Fellers, and Gramma Ruby too.

They met when Ruby Kiff was in her early twenties. J.P. was in his mid-forties, a widower with eight daughters and a stove and heating business in Toledo, Ohio. Five days a week she rode the canal boat into town to work at a spice company that gave away free dishes with each purchase. One day after work, walking back to the canal through rain that had been falling since morning, she saw that the grassy field she had to cross to get to the boat was now a sea of mud. Over her shoulder she heard a man's voice offering to help. Before she could turn around she was swept up, high off the ground, cradled in the man's arms, and was moving across the muddy field toward the boat waiting in the water in the rain. A few weeks later they were married. Ruby Kiff was now Ruby Fellers, the wife of a man more than twice her age and stepmother to his eight daughters. All, except for one, were older than she was. The nine of them became best friends and stayed best friends forever.

Three years after Ruby gave birth to my mother, J.P. got a call from a distant relative who was in the lumber business in South Carolina, saying he should come down and give it a try. He sold his stove and heating business, put Ruby, my mother, and a few possessions in the truck, and headed south. He moved them into a small house near the old sawmill he had bought sight unseen, rolled up his sleeves, and went to work.

He loved everything about his new trade, especially the time spent in the woods on the end of a two-man crosscut saw, bringing down huge trees and hauling them back to the mill to be cut into lumber. Ruby was up every morning before dawn, cooking breakfast and packing lunches for J.P. and the men before they headed out for the day.

The work was hard but life was good and the money was coming in nice and steady. Unfortunately it was going out as fast as it was coming in, because J. P. Fellers loved to gamble. Cards, dice, fistfights—he'd lay his money down. But he was going in the hole and the deeper he got the faster he dug, until he had run up some serious debts with some serious people. He packed up Ruby and my mother and left South Carolina late one night by the light of the sawmill burning to the ground. He was headed back north, where deep in the woods near the town of Napoleon, Ohio, the tree that would one day take his life was silently waiting.

He managed to scrape up enough money to buy the small sawmill on the edge of town and in time build a good strong house a stone's throw away. Most of his daughters now had husbands and children and were living nearby. Once again he was surrounded by family and friends, and once again he was the owner of a thriving business. My mother grew up and married a trumpet player who quit the band he was in and the road he was on when my sister was born. I was born three years later. We moved all over the state, but spent a lot of time in Napoleon with Grampa and Gramma Fellers.

My sister and I loved the sawmill. Grampa had built a sort of crow's nest in the corner of the mill about ten feet off the ground where we could sit and watch and listen to the song of the circular silver blur of a blade, the whine and the clang when it sliced into the length of a log, followed by an explosion of sawdust that shot into the air to the underside of the metal roof and then fell, along with the musical note of the blade, which rose again at the end of the run. One day a traveling artist came by. Grampa gave him a dollar and my sister and I sat on the hillside and watched him do a painting of the mill. It hung in the living room of the house from that day until many years after he had died.

I was four years old when Grampa Fellers died, and I don't remember when I heard the story of how it happened, but it started with him having gone out to look at some trees he was to cut down later in the week. That evening he told Ruby that there was one tree in particular he'd rather not have anything to do with. He said he didn't know why, but as he stood there that afternoon looking at it, sizing it up, he had the feeling the tree was doing the same to him. It wasn't the only time that week he said something to her about it, and she noticed he was having trouble sleeping at night. The day before he was to start the job, a man came to the mill and tried to convince him to buy a tool he said would make the life of a lumberman a whole lot easier. He said the day of the two-man crosscut saw was over. It was true that being on the end of one of those old saws was such backbreaking work the lumbermen called them "misery whips." He showed J.P. a brand-new chain saw and gave him a demonstration. J.P. thanked him but said he wasn't interested. The man said he could use it for a day for free, to see if he liked it, and handed him the saw.

Just before dawn as Grampa was leaving for work, Ruby told him good luck, not to worry, and that she would have his favorite meal waiting for him when he got home. Late that afternoon when the sun began to cool on the backside of the house she put the plates, cups, and silverware on the little table by the window at the far end of the kitchen. She walked back to the stove by the doorway, put some bacon grease in the pan, wiped her hands on her apron.

J.P. and his men had used the old crosscut saws to take down all the trees but one. The one that had been keeping him awake at night was still standing, the chain saw sitting at the base of it. He had good reason to be concerned about that tree and had done everything he could to try to make it fall exactly how, when, and where he wanted it to. He was especially concerned about how much weight there was at the top of it. Widow makers—that's what they called those limbs high up in the trees. And that damn chain saw—he didn't like it, didn't trust it, and didn't want to use it, but when one of his men stepped forward, eager to try it out, J.P. pushed him aside and grudgingly fired it up. From the start he hated the noise, the blue smoke, and the smell of the saw fouling the forest. The first few inches of the cut were no problem, but as the saw went deeper the tree began to resist and when it neared the heart, the tree refused. There was a fault in that massive wooden tower, and the vibration of the chain saw caused it to rupture and a thousand pounds of tree came down on J. P. Fellers, almost completely burying him in the earth. He was still alive but could not speak. He could not move. The men knew they couldn't free him and knew it was no use even to try when they saw his life leave his body through his eyes.

Ruby was standing at the stove, heating the bacon grease to cook the pork chops, when a strange feeling, one she had never felt before, started somewhere down inside her and worked its way up to the underside of her skin and out into the air. There was a hissing in her ears that grew until it sounded like locusts, then a high-pitched whine like a saw blade through oak, and then a sound from far away that was so loud it hurt. She looked over at the little table by the window and saw the fork that was sitting beside J.P.'s plate rise from the table, slowly move toward her, past her, through the doorway into the narrow room and come to rest on the seat of his rocking chair. At that very moment the phone on the small stand by the door rang. Ruby calmly picked it up and heard a voice say, "Ruby, J.P.'s dead." She said, "I know" and hung up the phone.

She ran the sawmill for several years after that, and did well with it, but when she was in her seventies she got an offer from a trucking company looking for space for parking. She sold to them and they tore down the mill. She quit driving in her mid-eighties, and moved into my mother's house in Bryan, Ohio. Once, while I was visiting from Oklahoma, Gramma and

I sat down and had a long talk. She was ninety years old and her health was finally failing. She told me without remorse or regret that she was ready to die. She said she had been blessed with a loving husband, eight stepdaughters, a daughter, two grandchildren, and eight great-grandchildren. Everyone from her generation and many from the one that followed was gone. She had outlived her time. The world had become a place she no longer understood. I was leaving town, and as I walked to my car I saw her sitting in the window in her rocker, wearing her thick glasses, reading the evening paper. She was holding it upside down. The next time I saw her she was in a pink dress, her eyes closed, her hair thin and silver, her head resting on a shiny pillow. She was ninety-one years old.

A few days later my mother and sister and I were cleaning out Ruby's house in Napoleon. We found drawers full of beautiful quilts and quilt scraps, boxes of sepia photos, and postcards from friends with very old postage stamps on them. There were newspapers from World War II; the entire front page of one was a gritty black-and-white picture of Pearl Harbor in flames.

We were sorting through old memories too when I said something about the strange story Gramma Ruby had told about the fork rising from the table, floating through the air, and coming to rest in the rocking chair the day Grampa died. I said that when I first heard it, whenever that may have been, I didn't know whether to believe it or not. Forks don't float. On the other hand, Gramma Ruby was not one to make up a story like that, or ever say anything that wasn't true. Both my mother and my sister said they had never heard that story, and my mother went on to say that Gramma had told her that on the day J.P. died she was in the kitchen making supper when she had a "premonition" someone was at the front door. When she opened the door she saw a man from the mill standing on the porch. She looked at him and said, "So it's true." He said, "Yes." She closed her eyes and let out one long scream, so loud and so shrill she was deaf in her left ear for the rest of her life.

I had no doubt that the story Gramma told my mother was true. And on that day, for the first time in my life, I began to wonder if I had made up the story I always thought Gramma Ruby had told me, maybe when I was just a kid, sparks from a saw blade striking a bit of metal, lighting the fuel of the imagination of a four-year-old grandson of a lumberman. Maybe it happened when my dad lifted me up and held me, leaning forward so I could see my grandfather. Black suit, white shirt buttoned at the neck, eyes closed, his bald head resting on a shiny pillow. So still. So quiet. The room barely breathing. Maybe then.

———

John Hadley

John Hadley was born in 1941 in Lisbon, Ohio. His father, who taught music in one-room rural schools, had a dance band and a machine that made acetate records. His mother and sister played the piano well, but not a note without the music. He says he never did learn to do that. They all played and sang into the machine, and he still has a cabinet full of those old 78s.

John and his family later moved west to a farm near Van Wert, Ohio. The school graduated about ten students a year. His dad was the superintendent, his history teacher, and the band director. His granddad Hadley was his math teacher, and his mother was the secretary. They then moved to Bryan,

Ohio, where he graduated from high school, going on to college in Athens, Ohio, and Madison, Wisconsin.

From 1965 to 1988 John taught art at the University of Oklahoma, and he went on from there to be a staff writer for the new Smothers Brothers Comedy Hour on CBS for two years. In 1991 he signed with Sony/ATV Music Publishing Inc.

Today John's family has grown to include his wife, Judi; sons, Jason, Jonas, and Josh; daughter, Jamaica; and grandkids, Ruby and Arlo. He's still doing the same thing he's done all his life: drawing and painting and writing songs. His songs have been recorded by a wide range of artists, including Roger Miller, Waylon Jennings, George Jones and George Burns, the Dixie Chicks, Tim O'Brien, Mollie O'Brien, David Olney, Kevin Welch, Kieran Kane, Trisha Yearwood, Garth Brooks, Wynonna, Linda Ronstadt and Ann Savoy, Joe Cocker, and others.

The Box

Kevin Welch

There was a box, a boot box, large and dusty and familiar, beneath the bed of a girl in love with being in love. There was a ribbon around it, saved over from a gift from a special boy, a basket of soaps and lotions and candies. She had almost forgotten where the ribbon had come from by now, but still it was important, because if it wasn't important, she wouldn't have saved it.

Inside the box were all the various love letters she had ever received from all the ones who had thought to write them to her, and every one was precious at the time, and never had she thrown a single one away. There were some that had revolted her, but she kept them anyway. Some had scared her a little, but she kept those too. Some had merely warmed her rather moist impression of herself, and were reassuring in their way. There were just a few down in that box, though, that were very private and very special, and these were the ones that she went to sometimes, late at night, to dig out and read and dream and weep and moan a little after the lights were out and no one would hear.

Years went by. The box aged with her, traveled with her too, from house to house, always staying under whichever bed she slept in. She rarely read from it anymore, though she would occasionally drop in a movie-ticket stub, a matchbook, a backstage pass, photos of good times, little reminders of nice evenings, special nights. Sometimes she would sift through it like a box of leaves, and maybe unfold one or another and let her eyes pass over the familiar words, the color of the paper, the old folds, and then let it resume its practiced shape, and replace the lid of the box with a sigh.

In time, she met a young man who she thought she loved. He began to sleep in the space above the box, in the girl's bed. Night after night, every night, he and the girl made love and slept, and finally it began to seem as if he would never leave, and she was happy.

One morning he woke up and couldn't find his shoes. He started looking all over the place, by the front door, by the couch, by the bed, under the bed. "What's in the box?" he asked.

"Oh, just letters and stuff."

He looked at her then, clearly, then dropped the bedspread down and stood and leaned and kissed her and went to work.

All day she thought about the box, and the look he had given her. Someday when she wasn't at home she knew he might decide to investigate. Maybe he was the beginning of a whole new life, maybe those old letters and snapshots would hurt him if he read them—should she just empty the box? But then he would wonder why it was missing.

Finally, she decided.

She pulled out the box and went through it, removing all the most special letters, the ones with the heat and the promises, being careful not to look at the handwriting, recklessly sorting aside the warmest memories, the fondest dreams, the wickedest fantasies. The photos, every handsome boy, every kiss caught in a moment and a flash, all set aside with a grim tremble and a blind resolve to do this thing before she thought about it one minute longer.

She carried these into the kitchen, raised the lid of the trash can, and ever so tenderly laid them on top of the pile of banana peels, coffee grounds, papers, and such. Gathering up the edges of the plastic bag, she tied it off and carried it out to the alley, where the big cans were overflowing, waiting for the pickup the next morning.

Back inside, she slid what was left of the box back under her bed, lighter and a little bit hollow. She felt better, she thought. Maybe she didn't. She couldn't tell; maybe she felt nothing at all.

Hour after hour she waited for him. Suppertime, then 10:00, then midnight, then 2:30, and she worried and she wondered where he could be?

3:30.

5:00.

And then she heard two sounds at the same time; the rumble of the morning garbage truck, and the front door opening.

There he stood with a look in his eye she hadn't seen before. Also a duck of the head and a shoulder hunch he'd never had. He wasn't looking at her right. He was radiating guilt.

And then everything shifted in her, just a sickening drop, and all of a sudden her head started humming and he was saying something but she missed it and then her hearing started coming back—and all she heard was a sound like wind in her ears and that garbage truck grinding down her alley, gone and gone and gone.

Kevin Welch

Born in Long Beach, California, on August 17, 1955, Kevin Welch traveled extensively till he was seven, when his family settled in Oklahoma. He made it through high school and one semester of music school at Central State in Edmond, Oklahoma, before he joined a bluegrass band, dropped out of school, and hit the road.

He met John Hadley, a real songwriter for Tree International, who also taught art at the University of Oklahoma. Hadley was immediately critical of his guitar playing, which made him try harder just to get even.

In 1978 he moved to Nashville with his new wife, Jennifer—like Hadley said they should—and started writing for Tree International. He had three kids, Dustin, Savannah, and Ada. Though Jennifer and Kevin split up, they remain good friends.

In the late 1980s, Steve Earle, Don Schlitz, Mark Germino, and some other madmen suggested that Kevin get a record deal; his friend Paul Worley went over to Warner Bros. and got Kevin signed. He made two records, Kevin Welch *in 1990 and* Western Beat *in 1992. Since Warner let Kevin do whatever he wanted, in 2004 he and his friends Kieran and Fats made a three-man record with no bass or drums, along with a companion record with their friend David Francey, the Scottish/Canadian poet and singer.*

Today, Kevin can usually be found in a chair in his office at home with a stiff neck, a warm PowerBook, and a cold cup of coffee. He lives with his beautiful and talented girlfriend, Claudia Scott, and they don't have one single pet. You can visit his Web site at www.kevinwelch.com.

A Rock

Kris Kristofferson

"Well I'll be go to hell!" my father said. He stood there with his hands on his hips and his Stetson pushed back far on his head.

Then Harve Ginn said, "I was checking the flood damage to see what we'd lost when I saw the damn thing. It must of been covered mostly with dirt and all before the water come up here."

"Well, I imagine there was some mesquite around here to cover it up before the flood. And you wouldn't notice it unless you came up on the right side of it anyway," my father said.

"No, I don't suppose you would at that," Harve said. "Boy, it's really something, though, isn't it?"

Well, I had to admit that it was really something, all right. I couldn't hardly believe my eyes when I saw it. What Harve had found was a big rock, oh Jeez, it must of been forty feet high, I guess. About the same size as the other big smooth rocks around there near the canyon wall. But this rock looked just like a big, naked woman. No kidding, that's just what it looked like. She was lying on her back, sort of leaning up against the canyon wall, in a kind of embarrassing way, and she had a sort of smile on her face. I'm telling you, I've never seen anything like it. My father kept saying, "Goddamn!" Like he couldn't believe it either. He and Harve decided that nobody could of done it. I mean made the thing, and that it must of always been there.

"It's just a freak of nature," I remember he said. Well I didn't care what it was, but I was sure going to let people know about it when we got back to town. I mean to tell you this was really some rock. I went up and rubbed my hand on it and it was rock all right. I think they say the rocks around there are some kind of granite.

"Come on, Kenny, get away from there," my father said.

"How come?" I said. "What's the matter with it?"

"I don't know," he said, "but I'm not sure it's such a good thing for a boy your age to be seeing."

Well that kind of stuck in my craw, and all the way home in the jeep I said "hell" and "damn" and talked as old as I could until I said, "That sure is a hell of a damn looking fence ol' man Palmer put up." They both stopped talking and looked at me, and I felt a little silly and didn't say anything else the rest of the way home.

When we pulled into the driveway my father said, "I'm going to call up Earl Bright from the *Herald* and take him out to see it."

I jumped out of the jeep and ran across the yard to the house. My mother was standing outside hanging up clothes and I said, "We found a big rock that looks like a naked lady," and I went into the house.

My father and mother followed me in, and my father was saying, "It's the damnedest thing you ever saw, a natural rock formation, and it looks like some sort of dirty statue." He was dialing the phone and said, "It's dang near thirty feet high—really a big thing," and my mother was saying, "What? What? What are you talking about?"

I said, "It's at least forty feet high, and it's a rock that looks just like a naked lady."

"Do you mean...all over!" she said, with a worried look.

"Yes." I was going to go on when my father motioned for us to be quiet.

"Hello, Earl?" he said. "This is Len Tipton. Howdy, yes, I'm fine. Say, we've run across a thing out here that you might be interested in looking at. I think it was uncovered by the flood. It's a big rock formation that's in the shape of a nude. Yeah, a woman. No, this is really big, and it looks as real as any sculpture." He listened for a while and said, "Well, actually, what it looks like is a prostitute," and he laughed, and my mother sent me out of the room.

Well, Earl Bright came out and he and my father drove back out to the rock and took pictures and things, and the next day there was a big story about it on the front page of the *Wheatonsville Herald*. Of course by this time the whole school knew about it and they all thought I'd found it and I guess I was sort of a hero. A lot of us went out to see it after school, those of us that had bikes, because that's just what everybody seemed to be doing. And when we got there, there were people all over the place. Why I'll bet half of Wheatonsville was there, and the other half on their way. They were all in a sort of half circle in front of it, staring, and pointing, and talking a mile a minute. A lot of the boys started making nasty remarks about it and laughing, and the women carried on something terrible. A lot of them acted mad, or embarrassed, and a few of them left, but most of them stayed.

Well, the crowds kept coming to see it for a few days, and the women never stopped talking about it. The way I understand it, some of them were downright mad, and said it was a disgrace and all. So they decided to call a town meeting and talk it over, and my father was supposed to go, seeing as how it was on our property, and I finally talked them into letting me go too. My mother said she didn't know if it was a thing for children, and my father said, "What the hell, he won't hurt anything," and so I went.

I'd never been to anything like that before, except maybe Sunday school. Everyone sat in rows facing up to the front of the church, which was where it was, and my father and I sat in the front row. The place was full of smoke, and hot, and everyone was red and sweating. They started right off when one man got up and said that something had to be done and he wasn't letting his children see that filthy goddamned thing and what were we going to do about it. And everybody started saying, "Yeah," and "That's right," and about then I decided I had to go to the bathroom, but I couldn't leave since I was in the front row and my father motioned me to be quiet every time I'd go to say something about it. Another man got up and said it was a slap in the face of every decent woman in Wheatonsville, and he looked red in the face and all hepped up like he wanted to fight somebody. I thought that over awhile, about the slap in the face, but I never did get what he meant.

Well they went on like that for quite a while, each one getting up and saying just about what the other had said and looking pretty pleased with himself when he finished. Then they all started saying, "What are we going to do?" and somebody said, "We could ask her at least to cross her legs," and everybody laughed. I tried to tell my father I was going to go to the bathroom, but he couldn't hear me for the noise. Then the man that had said that about the slap in the face got up, redder than ever, and yelled that maybe this was funny to a lot of people but he had a wife and three daughters and didn't think it was very funny. Well this quieted the room down just like that, just as I was bellowing to my father again that I was going to go to the bathroom. It was like bellowing at a funeral; and I was so ashamed I felt like never going to the bathroom again, but I went out anyway, and when I came back they were still going at it. Mr. Ludlow, the Baptist minister, got up and said that it was the something-or-other of Sin, and that any fool could see that, and that it was up to my father to do something about it, since it was on our property.

Well my father hadn't said anything as yet but I could tell he could've said plenty. He got up slow and said, "Look, this whole thing's getting out of hand. It's nothing to get excited about." He said it was just a natural rock, and it didn't seem to him there was anything anybody could or should do about it. If you didn't like it, he said, you shouldn't pay any attention to it. "I didn't ask anybody but Earl Bright to come see it, and no one has to see it that doesn't want to," he said.

A man got up and said, "How can we ignore it when that image of a leering strumpet is always over our shoulder? What kind of thing is that to show our kids?"

I didn't know what a strumpet was, but I agreed with him— it was a pretty hard thing to ignore. My father stood there, working his jaw like he does when he's about to blow up about something, but he didn't, and he said, "Well, let me know when you decide what to do." We stomped out of the church.

After that there were a lot of articles in the *Herald* about it, which my father read out loud to my mother, and it looked like they were hearing about *it* all over the state. More people than ever came to see it since the meeting, and the kids were always sneaking over to take a look. My father read us where a board of censors was studying it and that they weren't allowing any more pictures to be taken. One minister said it was made by God and couldn't be bad and we should leave it like it was, and some others followed him up—ones my father called "crackpots"—and tried to start a new religion about it. He said the nudists were claiming that it was proof that God was on their side, and that Billy Graham said it was proof that we were all going to hell.

Then one day a bunch of men and women came storming up in pickup trucks, and the men had guns. A man got out of the first pickup and I saw it was the man that had said that about the rock being a slap in the face, and he came up to my father and said, "Leonard Tipton"—which sounded funny because no one ever calls my father Leonard—"Leonard Tipton, since you refuse to do anything about this, we're taking matters into our own hands!" And he wheeled around and went blustering back to his pickup before my father could say anything. They all pulled out and went down the road to the rock, and pretty soon all the people started pouring out of there, and one of them told my father that the men with the guns had made them leave, and had set up a guard around it.

My father went into the garage and got the jeep, and I jumped in, and we drove to the rock. The men were standing pretty far from it with their guns, and my father pulled up the jeep. "Oh, for Christ's sake!" he said. I looked at the rock and saw that they had taken a great big canvas tarp and covered up all but the head of the woman. It really looked silly, I'll tell you, with that grinning head sticking over the top of the tarp. I'm not sure it didn't look worse than before. And they had the tarp staked down at the sides so it wouldn't come off. I thought it looked funny enough, but the men guarding it were serious, so I didn't laugh or anything. My father didn't say anything, he just put the jeep in reverse and we wheeled out of there.

Well the thing was up before the state council for about a week, and we weren't too popular around then. My father said the people were acting like idiots, and he quit talking to them and they quit talking to him. My mother said that maybe even if he was right, he ought to be sympathetic with the neighbors' feelings and tell them he'd do whatever they wanted him to do about it.

He said, "Oh, for Christ's sake, Alice, they've completely lost their senses. They're making this thing into some goddamned monster or something." Then he laughed and pointed to the newspapers. "Or if they're not doing that, they're practically worshipping it!"

He said, "It's only a rock!" and she said, "Oh, Len, do you always have to be so difficult?" and I said, "What's so only about a rock?" and they sent me to bed.

Well, we didn't have to worry about it for long, because some men from the state came up in trucks and one of them showed my father some papers and they drove back to the rock. They set up a bunch of dynamite and commenced to blast that rock until it didn't look like much of anything, and believe me, that was a show. So I guess that's about all there is to it and there's nothing there anymore. And everyone feels a little better. But when you think about it, and I don't guess I've thought much about anything else since they started making the fuss over it, that was some rock all right.

><del></del>

Kris Kristofferson

Born in Texas and raised in a military family, Kris Kristofferson was a Golden Gloves boxer who graduated Phi Beta Kappa from Pomona College in Califorina and earned a Rhodes scholarship to study literature at Oxford. He then served in the army as an Airborne Ranger helicopter pilot, achieving the rank of captain. In 1965, inspired by songwriters like Willie Nelson and Johnny Cash, he moved to Nashville to pursue his music.

Kristofferson achieved remarkable success in the early 1970s, writing such songs as "Me and Bobby McGee," "Help Me Make It Through the Night," "Sunday Morning Coming Down," and "For the Good Times," all chart-topping hits that helped redefine country songwriting. By 1987, it was estimated that more than 450 artists had recorded Kristofferson's compositions. The three-time Grammy winner has recorded twenty-six albums, including three with pals Willie Nelson, Johnny Cash, and Waylon Jennings as part of the Highwaymen, and his current CD, This Old Road.

Kristofferson has also acted in more than fifty films, including the Blade *trilogy,* Alice Doesn't Live Here Anymore, Pat Garrett and Billy the Kid, Fast Food Nation, Dreamer: Inspired by a True Story, *and* A Star Is Born, *for which he won the 1977 Golden Globe for Best Actor.*

Kristofferson is a member of the Country Music Hall of Fame, winner of the prestigious Johnny Mercer Award from the Songwriter Hall of Fame, and was honored with the American Veterans Association's "Veteran of the Year Award" in 2002. For Kristofferson's seventieth birthday in 2006, his friends and admirers gifted him with a tribute CD, The Pilgrim: A Celebration of Kris Kristofferson. *In 2007, Kristofferson was honored with the Johnny Cash Visionary Award from Country Music Television. You can visit his Web site at www.kriskristofferson.com.*

The Care and Treatment of Camp Cooks

Bob McDill

Amoment before, Spoony Odom had stood up from his place at the kitchen table and started toward the door. Dinner was over and the only duties left were washing the dishes and utensils, something Spoony never participated in. At the door he paused momentarily to untie his apron, as if he had forgotten it until just that moment. Then Beagle noticed him standing there, looking back at the men seated at the long kitchen table, waiting for recognition.

"Magnificient dinner, Spoony!" Beagle called out.

"Oh, thank you," the camp cook said, his face flushing.

"Yes, that one was over the top!" Beagle continued.

"Oh, you don't mean that," Spoony said.

"Those New Orleans chefs can take a backseat to you," Deacon Bidwell added. He pushed his chair back from the table to accommodate his broad stomach.

"You're all too kind," Spoony said, fumbling with his apron strings.

He was a small man, perhaps a size or two smaller than

the other club members, with fine silver-gray hair that he kept carefully combed. His facial features were well proportioned and almost delicate.

"By golly, you should open a restaurant!" the Deacon declared. The Deacon was always the first one to sit down for dinner and the last one to leave.

"Oh, go on," Spoony returned, turning a little red.

"No. I'm serious. You'd have people lined up around the block," the Deacon said. He had begun scraping the last of the chocolate mousse out of a pot on top of the stove.

Finally, when every compliment that could be thought of had been delivered, Spoony turned and left the kitchen. While the club members washed dishes, he sat alone by the fire in the TV room, sipping a tiny cup of espresso.

The Old River Rod and Gun, Bloody Mary Society and Gentlemen's Club wasn't the largest hunting camp around, nor did it offer the best shooting and fishing. But it had something no other club had. It had Spoony Odom. Among camp cooks, he was a legend. Spoony was no chili-and-beer man. Not by a long shot. He followed the New Orleans and European styles in culinary matters. He was a maker of sauces and stocks, a saucier. He had a flair for presentation. And he was a genius with desserts. Spoony was not a hired chef. With the stingy dues we paid at the Old River, we could never have afforded such a thing. He was a club member and cooked simply for the love of it, and, of course, for the adulation he received.

His menus were based on what was fresh and seasonal. Waterfowl were favored during the winter months and quail and dove (if enough could be collected) in autumn. In summer, he specialized in the fish that were plentiful in our reservoir. A camp favorite was pan-seared bass with maître d'hôtel sauce.

Simple side dishes of rice pilaf and sliced tomatoes with fresh basil usually accompanied it. He often paired this treat with a crisp chilled Chardonnay.

There are three rules concerning the care and treatment of camp cooks: Rule 1: No matter what the cook does or says, he's treated with groveling courtesy; Rule 2: The cook is never asked to perform any task other than cooking; Rule 3: The cook's food is never, ever criticized. We followed the first rule to the letter at the Old River. As for the second, we had no choice in the matter. Spoony knew his rights. If anyone had suggested he do something as mundane as help wash dishes, he would have been horrified. And as for painting or carpentry, it was out of the question.

But I did see the third rule violated once. Dawn had broken clear and cold over the marsh that Saturday morning. Duck hunting had been good that season and old blind No. 7 was filled with hunters. The night before, Spoony had put together a culinary masterpiece. It had begun with leek soup. The next course was grilled mallard breast with plum sauce, served with porcini mushroom risotto and wild mustard greens. It was all accompanied by a hearty Beaujolais. Dessert was New Orleans bread pudding. Obviously, Spoony felt he hadn't had enough praise the night before.

"How was the dinner last night, fellows?" he asked innocently.

Beagle decided to take the ball. He was a lawyer. If anybody could lay it on, it was Beagle.

"A magnificent repast, my friend!" he said.

"But what did you really think?" Spoony queried.

"A culinary masterpiece!" Beagle added.

"Really? Was it as good as usual?"

"Each one is more magnificent than the last," Beagle said, summing up.

"Well, I really want to know if there was anything amiss," Spoony said, dragging out the discussion.

"You do?" Pinky Lipscomb asked. Pinky removed his pork-pie hat and pushed back a shock of red hair as if gathering his thoughts.

"Of course," Spoony said.

"Well…" Pinky stammered.

"What is it?" Spoony asked.

"The soup was, was…a little salty," Pinky squeaked.

A collective gasp arose from everyone present.

"What?" Spoony asked, not sure he had heard correctly.

"The soup might have been a little salty," Pinky repeated.

There was a second gasp.

"Oh, boy. Now you've done it," the Deacon whispered from the back of the blind. And he had. Spoony turned as cold and silent as the South Pole. For the rest of the morning, he looked off at the horizon as if he were searching the sky for ducks. When spoken to, he was curt and sullen. After reconsidering, Pinky apologized, saying he'd been wrong about the soup.

"No, no," Spoony snapped back. "I'm sure you're right. I suppose it was terrible."

By cocktail hour his mood hadn't changed. At seven he was sitting alone in the TV room and had made no move to start dinner. If it hadn't been for the hundreds of new ducks that had poured into our fields that afternoon on the heels of a cold front, he might have left the club in a huff.

The rest of us huddled in the kitchen.

"Well, what was I supposed to say?" Pinky asked, defending himself.

"You know how Spoony is," the Deacon scolded. "Why did you have to open your big pudding hole?"

"Well, he asked us, didn't he?" Pinky whined. "He wanted to know if anything was wrong."

"Since when did you become a soup expert, anyway?" the Deacon continued. "When you joined this club, you didn't even know what a leek was."

Finally the group came to a decision. They decided that I was to be their spokesman.

"You're his friend," the Deacon pleaded. "You can talk to him."

I was not aware that I was Spoony's friend, that is, any more or less than the other members. After all, Spoony was a difficult man. But off I went, representing the whole membership, knowing that a lifetime of canned chili and saltines might lie ahead of us. When I entered the TV room he was sitting in his favorite chair staring at the fire.

"Evening, Spoon," I said in a cheerful voice.

"Evening," he said sullenly.

"It's getting on towards dinnertime, Spoon," I hinted.

"Oh, I won't be cooking tonight," he answered.

"Why not, Spoon? If it's Pinky, I can—"

"Oh no," he interrupted. "Just don't feel up to it, you see."

I passed the bad news on to the others. That night each of us made himself a cold sandwich. The big table in the kitchen looked strangely bare with only cheese, sandwich meat, and a few other things dotting its long surface. Spoony's chair, normally the one closest to the stove, was conspicuously empty. Only the week before, he had prepared his goose and sausage gumbo. The smell and taste of it was still fresh in my memory. The roux had been rich and dark, the sausage spicy, and the goose succulent. There was a salad of baby greens and fresh watercress. Two loaves of hot french bread were passed around the table.

That year turned out to be above average for duck hunting. Spoony continued to show up at the club every weekend but he went nowhere near the kitchen. He cleaned his birds carefully as always and put them in the freezer. The Deacon claimed that he had seen him eating a turkey on brown bread sandwich in his car. Beagle tried to appeal to his vanity.

"A man of your great talent, my friend, has a duty to his companions and to his club—indeed to the world!"

But Spoony claimed that he had lost interest in cooking. He went on to say that thirty years devoted to the pursuit and perfection of a single art were probably enough. Furthermore, he was now considering taking up the five-string banjo. Some of the members actually began considering staying home with their families on weekends. Finally Beagle came up with a plan. It was a long shot, but it was all we had. We cornered Pinky and laid out the details.

"I'm just not comfortable with this," he said, protesting.

"Why not?" Beagle asked.

"Well, for one thing, its not honest."

"I wouldn't quite call it dishonest," Beagle said.

"But I'd be telling a lie."

"I wouldn't quite call it a lie," Beagle added.

"Look. I won't say Spoony and I are close or anything, but it just wouldn't be right, making up this cockamamie story and all."

"Think of the members," the Deacon pleaded.

"No. I really don't think I can do it," Pinky said.

"Look," the Deacon demanded, "you can fish, can't you?"

"Yes."

"Then you can lie."

"Okay, okay," Pinky said, holding up his hands in surrender.

He found the camp cook in the kitchen, ceremoniously packing his spices into a cardboard box.

"Spoon?" he began carefully.

"Yes?" Spoony answered.

"There's something you ought to know," Pinky said. "I've been telling some of the fellows and, well, you see…"

"What is it?" Spoony asked impatiently.

"I've sort of run into a rough patch," he said.

Spoony stared at the label on a bottle of coriander and said coolly, "Oh? What kind of rough patch?"

"It's my health, Spoon."

"It's your heart, isn't it?" Spoony responded. "I've told you before, all you fellows eat too much fat."

"No, no, it's not my heart," Pinky said, pausing for effect. "I've been hiding this from you and the other members. But I can't hide it any longer. It's my brain."

"Your brain?" Spoony asked, looking up.

"Yes, you see I've been diagnosed with a…disorder." He looked at Spoony carefully, trying to judge his reaction.

Spoony was caught off guard. "Disorder?" he asked.

"Yes."

"Well, h-h-how bad is it?" Spoony stammered.

"I'm afraid it's pretty bad. Soon I'll have to surrender most of my mental faculties," Pinky said, as if reading from a medical textbook.

"Oh," Spoony said, his eyes growing wide.

"Yes. And then I'll be…well, you know."

"Well, how long do you have?" Spoony asked.

"Not long, I'm afraid," Pinky said, gaining confidence. "You see, once the symptoms start, it's just a matter of—"

"What symptoms?"

"Loss of sensory integrity."

"What?"

More sure of himself now, Pinky went on. "All the senses start to short out. You know: hearing, smelling."

"I've never heard of anything like that," Spoony said, suspiciously.

"It's new," Pinky said.

"So you're telling me all your senses are going haywire and now your hearing and your smelling and your vision and your—" Spoony stopped in midsentence. A look of enlightenment came into his eyes. Then they narrowed as if he might be attempting to resolve some difficult dilemma. Finally, as Pinky jabbered on, an expression of peace settled across Spoony's face. Perhaps his refusal to cook had gone on long enough. Maybe he was being offered a way to return to the bosom of his friends, a way simply to put things back the way they were. Whatever his thoughts, they went unnoticed by Pinky. He was now going on tearfully about how his sweet wife, the love of his life, now smelled like creamed corn.

Spoony turned to him and offered his hand.

"Yes, yes, quite tragic," he said, with a faint smile. "And what you said about the soup, let's . . . forget it."

When Pinky returned to the TV room, he plopped into a chair and let out a long breath. "I think he bought it," he said.

That evening the camp cook went back to his saucepans. The members were unusually quiet as we gathered in the kitchen for drinks. All eyes were on Spoony as he began preparing dinner. But Spoony was quiet too. He tiptoed around the room as if he might be afraid of spoiling his return to the fraternity of the club. But then the Deacon began ribbing one of the newer members about not making a shot all morning. I glanced over at Spoony. He was grinning appreciatively. Soon the level of noise and laughter rose as the men relaxed into a familiar old pattern. Someone had contributed some Georgia quail to the larder, and Spoony rubbed them with rosemary and garlic and flambéed them in cognac. There were also steamed asparagus and garlic grits. When dinner was put on the table, we all went at it like starving jackals—all except for Pinky, who pretended only to pick at his plate. But when Spoony's back was turned, he wolfed down huge mouthfuls. After a dessert of rice pudding with bourbon sauce, we pushed back our chairs. Beagle lit a cigar. The conversation turned, as usual, to weather and water-fowl. Finally, someone broke the spell.

"Well, those dishes aren't going to wash themselves."

The camp cook immediately stood up and started toward the door. But when he reached it, he stopped. Then, as if he had just at that moment remembered his apron, he turned, fac-ing the men seated at the long table, and began fidgeting with the apron strings. Beagle saw him first.

"Absolutely wonderful dinner, Spoon!" he called out, lean-ing back in his chair.

"Oh, you don't mean that," the camp cook said, blushing with pleasure. "Do you?"

Bob McDill

Bob McDill is a retired songwriter and music publisher. During his long career he wrote thirty-one number-one songs, as well as songs for movies and television. His movie credits include The Thing Called Love *and* Primary Colors. *He was elected to the Nashville Songwriters Association Hall of Fame in 1985 and is the only Nashville songwriter ever to be voted Writer of the Year by both Broadcast Music Inc. and the American Society of Composers, Authors and Publishers.*

He has lectured on music and Southern culture at the University of South Carolina and at Lamar University and was prominently featured in Nobel laureate Sir V. S. Naipaul's book A Turn in the South. *He now works as a freelance magazine writer and has written articles and stories for several national publications.*

Bob is a member of the Coffee House Club, a Nashville men's club that began in 1909. He sits on the William G. Hall Scholarship committee at Belmont University. He assisted in fund-raising for Vanderbilt Children's Hospital in 1985 and 1988. He is a past member of the Nashville Board of Governors of NARAS as well as a former member of the ASCAP advisory board and a supporter of Nashville Opera and Tennessee Repertory Theater. He was named a distinguished alumnus of Lamar University in 1989. His biography appears in the 1991–1992 editions of Who's Who in the South and Southwest *and* Who's Who in the World.

A Big Batch of Biscuits

John Bohlinger

When social services contacted her about the food drive, Martha dreaded the ordeal. She had to meet her caseworker once a month and that was bad enough. She hated sitting, or sometimes standing, in that crowded waiting room with all those angry women, vacuously staring at the snowy, deafening TV in the corner while their dirty children tore through the old magazines on those filthy tables, or picked up the worn blocks in the play center and lifted them with sticky, fat fingers into their drooling mouths. Martha always felt too depressed to be horrified. How did she get here? She was nouveau poor, completely unprepared for this unexpected chapter in her life. She'd spent her youth learning about art and culture. She could speak some French, scan poems, and identify the artwork of masters, but now dealing with food stamps, Medicaid, and Section Eight housing seems wildly complicated. Yet here she sits, surrounded by uneducated teenage mothers who are amazingly adroit at working through this complex labyrinth of red tape.

She hates the other women here. Martha always brings a

book to SS so she can avoid eye contact or, worse, a conversation with the other mothers. She never chooses easy books, either. Today she's reading *Paradise Lost,* which seems like a perfect choice not only because of the obvious irony, but it's a collegiate read that will show the staff, other mothers, and herself that, although she is down on her luck, she is not one of them. She is normal; a former soccer mom.

Martha thinks about the soccer moms at her kids' school in their new SUVs, with perfect figures and blond helmet hair. She imagines them reading about the food drive in the school flyers, walking through their enormous, clean kitchens to their well-stocked walk-in cupboards and loading cans of solid white albacore tuna, mushrooms, fruit, snow peas, and bottles of olive oil into the food-drive bags. Maybe there will be a can of baby corn, water chestnuts, cashews, and a box of rice with which Martha could improvise a nice stir-fry for the kids. It wouldn't be quite like she used to make, but it would have to do until next month's food stamps come through.

The desk calls out names and women trudge to the front to collect their food. They grab their two allotted bags without a word of thanks, yell for their kids, and leave angry. Although Martha has seen this behavior often over the past months, the rudeness still shocks her.

"SPALDING, MARTHA!"

"Yes." Martha sounds overly cheerful. She wants to set an example for the others, but that might have been a little too sugary.

"Sign here."

"Here…okay. Thank you very, very much. Have a great day."

"You're welcome, honey. SPEARS, JANELL!"

Martha hoists her two bags of groceries up on her hips and heads toward the door. *They're pretty heavy—that's good,* she thinks as she shoulders the door open.

Outside she sees bags of flour and cornmeal littering the sidewalk. "Unbelievable," Martha says to herself. "Not only are these people ungrateful, they're stupid. They're too lazy to carry this perfectly good food home. No wonder they're poor. Rich people don't waste food like this." She's tempted to pick up some of the food and sneak it to her car, but there are some other women standing there and Martha is too embarrassed. She rests the bags on the hood of her Corolla, unlocks the door, and places the bags on the floor in back where they won't fall over. Martha slides behind the wheel, fires up her car, and begins driving home. For the first few blocks she passes a slow, dotted line of mothers and children from SS. Children walk precariously close to the busy street carrying cans of food while their mothers, balancing bags and babies, languidly march until they eventually disappear into the maze of projects. Martha thanks God that she still has a car. These food-drive bags are heavy.

While Martha drives home she thinks about what she will cook. She imagines the kids coming home to their little apartment and she greets them with some fresh biscuits. Maybe even with a little honey butter. Martha remembers how her ex used to love her biscuits. She pictures their old home, which now seems palatial compared to her current Section Eight apartment. The fifteen-minute drive goes quickly when lost in a daydream of her former life. It really was a dream, and at times a nightmare. David was getting worse and she knew she might not be as lucky next time.

As she unlocks her front door, Martha thinks about her Calphalon copperware and wonders where it is now. When you're fleeing for your life, you just don't think about pots and pans. She had to get the essentials packed for her and the kids, pick them up from school, and get out of town before David got off work. She was so worried that he might stop home for some reason, although he never had in the past. The truth is, he hadn't even called from work for the past year. Martha now wishes she had taken the time to pack just one good frying pan and a cookie sheet, but that's the thing about running for your life: everything but survival seems petty.

The daydream spell breaks as Martha begins to unload her treasured groceries. Five cans of Kroger creamed corn, three cans of Kroger string beans, a forty-ounce can of spaghetti sauce, a five-pound sack of flour, a jar of grape jelly, a can of Morton salt. If she can borrow some vegetable oil and baking powder from her neighbor—they've spoken a little bit in passing and she does seem nice—this might be a good icebreaker. What was her name? Patty? Peggy? Doesn't matter—she'll borrow a cookie sheet, just a bit of vegetable oil, or margarine, or maybe butter if she's lucky. Plus she'll need baking powder if Peggy/Patty has it. She'll make a big batch of nice hot biscuits and give some to the neighbor to pay her back. That might start a nice friendship; her first friend in her new life.

As Martha opens the flour sack, she's confronted with mealworms writhing in the sudden light. Martha jumps back, dropping the sack, and watches in horror as the bugs twist in the spilled flour on the stained kitchen counter. When the kids get home two hours later, Martha is still sitting on the kitchen's linoleum floor. She wipes her eyes on the back of her hand, smiles, and says brightly,

"Hi, kids, how was your day?"

John Bohlinger

*A native Montanan and a Phi Beta Kappa graduate of
Columbia University, John Bohlinger has worked as:*

*a teacher/counselor in an orphanage in Honduras,
an Alaskan cannery fish slimer,
a pawnbroker,
a part-time faculty member of Eastern Montana College,
    teaching freshman composition and deliberative writing,
a dishwasher,
a tree surgeon,
a roofer,
a waiter,
a Ph.D. candidate in psychology,
a census taker for the year 2000,
a bread-truck diver,
a carpenter,
a songwriter,
a musician,
and (please forgive him) a telemarketer.*

*Since 2002, John has been the band leader for the USA/NBC
Network's hit program* Nashville Star. *He tours nearly
continuously, playing mandolin, pedal steel, and guitar for
dozens of major label artists.*

    *John's music compositions can be heard in several major
motion pictures, on major label albums, and in over one
hundred television spots. Mr. Bohlinger may be the only person*

currently working in television today who cuts his own hair. He and his life partner, Budzo the mixed-breed mutt, reside in Nashville.

His latest album, Djongo Solo, *is available from Farm2Market Records.*

Shiny, Like New

Dony Wynn

In the strange and cockeyed heart of central Louisiana is a town that is situated just north of swamps and cypress and directly south of rolling hills and pines: Alexandria. Here in this tiny blip on the map—a devoid, listless no-man's-land—two car salesmen are standing on the showroom floor of Alexandria Lincoln Mercury, admiring a brand-new 1972 Lincoln Mark IV, aqua with white leather trim, oohing and aahing over the new aerodynamic design but grumbling about the $8,400 price tag, remarking that "no one will pay this much for a car! It will never sell!"

During the salesmen's customary morning discourse, a caffeine-addled dismantle and harangue of the world at large, an old black man walks through the front showroom door clothed in dirty, tattered bib overalls, a denim shirt with the sleeves rolled up, and construction boots caked with dried red clay.

Bud, one of the salesmen, wears nothing but a tight-lipped smile and a gaudy assortment of polyester plaids. He's color-blind and has never told anyone; everyone just assumes he exercises bad taste. It's only a quarter of ten and Bud's already polished off a pint of Old Grand Dad. Averting his gaze from the old black man to give full concentration to the tops of his plastic brogans, Bud belches softly and swallows some acid backwash.

Jim is the other salesman. Lizard lipped, divorced three times, and not presently dating through any choice of his own, he chain-smokes unfiltered Viceroys that accentuate perpetual halitosis while gobs of dandruff litter the drooping shoulders of his maroon leisure suit. Blood pressure averages 190/110. A cigarette dangles from clenched yellowed teeth, blue lips pulled back in a permanent grimace. His eyes, reptilian slits, caustically watch the old black man hobble past on bowed legs.

A bogue, a squirrel, for sure, Bud and Jim both concur, giving each other the all-knowing smirk. Figuring it to be a waste of their invaluable time, they continue to ignore the old black man and harrumph! and pshaw! and ffeu! It will never sell!

Don, the newest salesman on the force, leaps up from his desk—a little too enthusiastically—introduces himself, and vigorously shakes a thick ham hock of a hand. Recently engaged, he's buried with high-interest loans from both a furniture and a jewelry store to prepare for his fiancée crossing his threshold till death they do part. His family assured him it was a step in the right direction. He feels the heat.

"Mah wife never axe for nothin'—no new dress, no popcorn or candy at the movin' pichures, no fur or jewry stones," the old black man says matter-of-factly. "Just some monries to put in the offerin' plate at Sunday meetin'." He stops and stands beside by the Mark IV. "But we pass by here the other day and she said she sho' nuff liked this here shiny new automobile." Old black man bends down and squints, examining the price tag taped inside the driver-door glass. Squeezing two fingers into his uppermost pocket, he says, "Manage to squirrel 'way somes after I sold mah fahm to Missir Charlie White, that developin' man."

Bud and Jim watch in stunned silence as the old black man pulls wads of crumpled one-hundred-dollar bills out of every conceivable pocket in the overalls and places them in Don's outstretched hands.

"I wants to buy this here cah for mah wife. I loves to see her smile."

The old black man has the car delivered to his house that afternoon. His wife is afraid. "I don't even have no license!" she argues. Won't even sit in it. Instead she yelps and claps her hands and hugs her husband more times than he can count. She runs in circles until she is dizzy, but the aqua 1972 Lincoln Mark IV with white leather interior stays in the carport, odometer stuck on twenty-three.

Old black man washes and polishes the car every now and then, tinkers with the plugs, runs the engine to keep the oil circulated, keeps the air pressure in the tires a constant. "You never knows," he'll say. "You might jump up 'n' drive this cah right on outta here one day. Yessah, drives it all the way to Timbuktoo." Meanwhile, his wife, tittering and twaddling all the while, sits in it, pretending to drive; fussing with the car's quadraphonic radio, clicking the blinker, tilting the driver's seat every which a way, making the tinted moon-roof glide back and forth, squealing with delight when it glides back and lets the midday sunshine flood in. Pops open the trunk with the magic button in the glove box. Inspects her flawless caramel skin in the visor's lit vanity mirror, her face framed by soft, golden halos. Looking every bit a stranger, she is quiet, observing features in the mirror's glow that are foreign to her. She touches her fingers to her cheeks to see if it is indeed her that is staring back. She is combustible. Eat up.

The old black man rubs the chromed front grille in bemused silence, enjoying his wife's antics to the bone.

When leaves fall and trees stand naked, resolute, and gnarled, lizard-lipped Jim suffers a fatal stroke. Two very drunk drinking buddies and his third ex-wife are the only ones to show up for the funeral. The mortician used red lipstick to infuse some life into his flattened blue lips. There is no will, which has infuriated the third ex-wife, who curses him aloud at the service. There is no headstone at the gravesite. More leaves fall and the wind blows a little harder, a little colder, laying bare all that is left in its wake.

After traveling from one used-car lot to another, each one worse than the last, Bud still favors plaid, polyester clothes. Cheaper ones now. Is up to a fifth of any inexpensive bourbon a day. He is not frugal, just broke. One afternoon, on his lunch break, he comes home to his empty trailer on the outskirts of town, pours himself a triple shot of Drano. Keeps him in ICU for two months; his throat and parts of his stomach burned away. No one appears to care. He never has so much as a visitor from the outside world. Kate, his only daughter—divorced and living in Indio, California—sends him flowers, but never calls. Only one nun from St. Francis Cabrini comes by—just once—and finds every excuse thereafter to keep from having to do it again, feeling her faith being siphoned into his black-hole dread; the nun's faith is later brought into question, causing her eventually to leave the diocese confused. The used-car lot where he works goes belly-up while he's recovering from his fourth surgery to rebuild his esophagus. His thoughts aren't on *I ain't in the mood for no jickey jack, you hear! What's your bargain basement price? Your absolute bottomest dollar?*

The Earth continues to twirl and spin and the 1972 Lincoln Mark IV, still shiny, like new, sits immobile in the garage, twenty-three miles on the odometer. A charcoal northern wind coaxes thunderheads over the Red River, into town, swallowing the last shafts of sunflower and puce emanating from an evaporating sun.

Arm in arm, the old black man and his wife stroll along the central hallway of the Greater Alexandria Mall. Stopping to admire the glamorous window displays of Weiss and Goldring Department Store, she gazes longingly at a nondescript, beaded, black purse. Noticing the price tag, she gasps. The price is *Mo' money than some peoples makes in a month!* Tugging on his arm to whisk him away, she whispers in his ear, "That there puss is the mos' beautimous thing I ever seen—an' the mos' ridikulus."

After a quick glance at the price tag, the old black man mutters, "Jew sto'." But even he has to admit *That puss is some kinda faincy....Bootiful, like fo' a queen.*

A short time later—after money is proffered, pleasantries exchanged—she clutches the beaded black purse to her bosom as her husband holds open the front door of the theater where *The Blues Brothers* is playing, a new movie whose previews had made her laugh out loud when they were watching television last night after dinner.

He pays the five-dollar admission for the two of them and says to her, "I think I'd like me a sodee pop."

She walks by his side to the concession stand. He orders the drink, then turns and asks his wife, "Would you like sometin', dear?"

Shifting her weight from foot to foot, she ponders the candy and all the bright, colorful wrappers, the smell of fresh-popped popcorn, the soft drink machine foaming and gurgling. She casually chews on the end of her fingernail and finally says,

"Honey, you jus' too good to me, drivin' me here in that big ol' faincy cah 'n' all." She brushes some lint from his shoulder. "And I got me a puss prettier than mos' everything I ever done seen. No...I's fine. I don't need nothin'. Besides"—she pulls at his collar to take out a crease and flicks more smutz from his shoulder—"what else is there?—'ceptin you?"

The old black man reaches over and affectionately strokes his wife's cheek. He takes a mouthful of his drink, loudly sucking the carbonated pop through the red-and-white-striped straw. It's cold. And syrupy. And his teeth sting.

The aqua Lincoln Mark IV with the white leather trim sits out front in the theater parking lot. Still shiny. Like new. On the passenger seat is a card that is open. Face up. It reads:

Damascus and Pearline—
Congratulations on your 40th wedding anniversary. Thank you, again, for walking into my life and forever changing it.

I'm now New Car Manager at Alexandria Lincoln Mercury. Come by and see me whenever you need a new one, or just stop in and say, "Hey!"

All the best,
Don

In a blustering wind that sweeps the parking lot clean, the 1972 Lincoln Mark IV has fifty-three miles on the odometer now. The engine is warm.

Damascus doesn't enjoy the film on the whole. Too damn loud, but he loves it when Aretha sings in the restaurant. He remembered where he was the day he first heard Aretha sing "Respect"—walking across the parking lot of Top's Bar BQ in Memphis, Tennessee, on Poplar Avenue, sandwich in hand, a mouth stuffed full of pork and slaw, sauce dripping down his chin. He could still taste the pungent juices of the smoked meat, the sweet crunch of the slaw, and he could feel the bounce in his step hearing the voice of the Queen of Soul blasting from the outdoor speakers, "R-E-S-P-E-C-T, find out what it means to me," just like it was yesterday.

Pearline laughs throughout the movie, holding on to her new purse as if her life depended on it. Her stomach pains her, but she does her best to ignore it and laughs till she cries, tears melting down her face, over hands that try to conceal sniffles, providing balm for the hurt that burns her deep, farther than she can ascribe or comprehend.

When they leave, Damascus holds open the theater doors for his wife and the dank night air rushes in, taking her breath away, making his eyes water. She flings her floral cardigan over her shoulders and hugs her chest.

As one, they walk across a parking lot pocked with light, a light that erases and blots the darkness that seeps like ink, devouring the dingy, stagnant town if only for a night. He vows to tell his wife of her tumor first thing in the morning. The doctor had given him the news a few days ago, abdicating to his wishes for him to be the one to tell her. Further tests need to be conducted to see if the grapefruit-sized tumor in her abdomen is malignant, or benign, but the words haven't found a way out of him yet. Whenever he works up the courage to tell her, the words wrap around his chest and his throat and squeeze the very air from his lungs, silencing him as if an invisible, formless thief has stolen away with the means quite unexpectedly. He invokes God. He feels trepidation. Any minute he will fall facefirst off the cliff's edge and be dashed to nothingness.

Pearline looks at him, knowing full well and why, and says, "I sure do loves you, you hurly-burly ol' main," and plants a full, plum-lipped kiss on his scratchy cheek, a four-day growth rasping her chin, the tip of her nose tingling from the bristle of his whiskers.

He opens the car door for her. She slides onto the leather seat and looks up at her husband. Damascus smiles at her. A crooked smile. Pearline smiles back, a smile so big and wide a pair of half-moon dimples escape the clouds momentarily and frame her dark chocolate eyes, eyes that glow with an inner fire all their own, embers smoldering with the manna of the ages.

"Honey?" he says.

"Yeah?" she says.

"I jus' loves to see you smile." Then he shuts the car door with care, taking note of the solid, reassuring clunk that makes him feel safe, protected.

The silence is broken by a chorus of laughter; two white teenage couples are walking hand in hand in the parking lot, carefree, their heads thrown back, mouths open wide, letting freedom ring and ring and ring. Lit roman candles. All full up, swollen to bursting.

Walking around the front of the car to the driver's side, Damascus runs his hand over the burning cold of the chrome bumper and grows older ... and more afraid.

Pearline opens the vanity mirror. She studies her eyes, her aquiline nose, her brace of straight, white teeth, and thinks, *I nevah felt mo' 'live,* and giggles at a reflection she now recognizes, her dimples healing a blind world. *On a mission from Gawd? ... Ohhh my lands ...*

><del>

Dony Wynn

Dony Wynn was born in the year of 19-and-56 to Don and Barbara Jean Wynn. They raised him good. Proper like.

Whilst still in diapers, listening to 45s with his folks, he was ceremoniously struck a wicked blow courtesy of a rhythm stick. Because of his natural proclivity thereafter for beats and such, he left the familial nest earlier than most, traveling, living dang near all over the globe for the better part of twenty years or so, smackin' drums and gleanin' a world-class education under the tutelage of one singin' fool, master in the art of living well, Robert Palmer. Spent a fair amount of time makin' butts move with Dr. John, Steve Winwood, Blondie, Patti LaBelle, Wang Chung, and Brooks & Dunn, too. He still makes a racket now and then when he feels so inclined, so inspired.

He lives in Austin, Texas, now. Plumb happy about that. Had disappeared from the world for an extended period and returned to civilization diversified and emboldened, finding himself now serving the cruel mistress that is music in a variety of ways and means whilst he has added pounding his computer keyboard with nary a grain of mercy, seriously gettin' all his yayas out, as is his wont, his need.

Alas, the creative flood, she will not abate.

He wonders what trouble woulda befell him—and, in turn, the public at large—if he didn't beat on somethin' all this lifetime? Goodness gracious. Lordy. The mind reels....

The Clock Struck Nine

Hal Ketchum

Marta woke before dawn. She lay still, her eyes closed. Her hands were folded across her chest. She listened to the old house sigh in the stillness. All was right in the world. She rose, dressed, crept past her parents' room, out the door, into the street.

She crossed the square, saw no one but an old man and a pack of dogs.

Three streets down, she slipped into a house.

Twenty minutes later she walked to the corner, boarded the seven-o'clock bus.

She paid the driver and went to the back.

She rode in a strange silence. The world had stopped and she alone had continued.

As time passed, the landscape changed from sparse villages to congested housing projects. With each stop, a few more people boarded. College students, businessmen, a woman in mourning clothes. No one looked at her.

She was invisible. Already gone.

The bus entered the city. Marta checked her watch.

7:52.

She quickly calculated, determined that she had plenty of time to reach her destination. She had to be inside the train station by nine o'clock. That's when she would explode.

She felt under her robes. The package taped there felt cold against her skin. Nineteen years old and already a holy warrior. Her thoughts went to the glory of her cause; she tried to hold them there. Sadly, she could only do so for a few seconds at a time. No matter how she tried, she could not erase the vision of her parents in tears.

After a few more stops, she realized the bus was no longer moving. She looked out the front, saw rows and rows of dirty vehicles going nowhere. She decided to leave the bus and walk. Just ten blocks to the station.

She wove her way along the busy street. Moved in rhythm with the people she intended to kill. She averted her eyes as she passed two soldiers. Up ahead, through the crowd, she could see the station.

8:32.

She pressed on, caught up in her own doom.

8:47.

Up the stairs, through the doors, into the station.

She stood for a moment and scanned the great hall.

She saw the fountain below the large clock. The ideal spot.

8:52.

She wove her way through the innocent, as if they were standing still. Ghosts of ghosts. Tall men, porters, mothers, babies.

8:55.

She reached the fountain feeling exhilarated.

She turned. Something hit her from behind. She watched an old woman sprawl across the floor. The contents of her bag sailed through the air, landing at Marta's feet. Marta bent down, gathered the old woman's belongings. The old woman knelt before her and smiled.

8:57.

Marta panicked. She tried to look away. But the old woman's eyes held her.

Suddenly life seemed more sacred than death. In a single motion, Marta reached beneath her robes and pulled at the wires on the hidden explosives.

There would be no sorrow today.

Marta met the old woman's gaze with a smile.

The old woman became pure light and vanished.

The clock struck nine.

❧

Hal Ketchum

Hal Ketchum blazed onto the music scene in the early 1990s, when he struck record gold with his first single, "Small Town Saturday Night," which shot to number one on the country charts. Since then, he has had fifteen top-ten hits, sold over four million records, and has had his songs recorded by artists ranging from Neil Diamond to Trisha Yearwood. Recently Hal said, "I love my live shows, getting in front of my people, they give me the drive and enthusiasm to make more music." In 1994, Hal became a member of the Grand Ole Opry, and he often hosts the television show Opry Live, *which airs on Saturday nights on the Great American Country Network (GAC), with his "Opry Family."*

Hal lives in Nashville with his wife of ten years, Gina,

and their three children, Fani Rose, Ruby Joy, Sophia Grace, and their dog, Sam. Rumor has it that his is the only estate in Nashville with a tomahawk target field, for the man of the house to get his practice in when he comes off the road to relax and unwind with a friendly "game of throwing hawks." He also works on his other passion: art. Since his original artwork sold out at his first gallery show in Sante Fe, New Mexico, in 2004, Hal has pursued his art by illustrating a children's book series with Gina. You can visit his Web site at www .halketchum.com.

Of Guitars & Righteous Men

Janis Ian

"There are men who steal silver, and men who steal gold
"But the worst kind of thief is the man who steals your soul."

It started with my father, who made the transition from chicken farmer to music teacher when I was around three.

Actually, it started with my dad's membership in various socialist organizations, since he needed a guitar to take to the meetings when he led them in singing.

No, I guess it started before that, when he bought The Guitar.

He bought it in 1948, from the widow of a farmer who'd had it lying around in the attic for years. When she asked what Dad thought it was worth, he replied "I dunno—twenty-five bucks?" He brought it home three years before I was born, and began learning to play. It was rural New Jersey; there weren't exactly a lot of other guitarists around. Somehow, he got a Weavers songbook with chord diagrams, subscribed to *Sing Out!* magazine, and we were on our way.

I grew up with that guitar. It was miles too big for me, a

colorful, beat-up window into another world. My small fingers could barely fit around the neck. As I began learning chords, I discovered new ways of fingering them to compensate for my size. To this day, I play a D chord "wrong." By the age of eleven, I was arguing over technique; when we went to see friends whose sons played with fingerpicks and they insisted that was what "real" guitarists did, I just sneered.

It helped that The Guitar went everywhere with us: to summer camp, where my father obtained eight-week stays for his children by teaching music for nothing; to my grandparents', where we went every weekend to pick up groceries from my grandfather the bagger. It went with Dad to work, it went with us to play.

The guitar you grow up with, the guitar you learn to play on, is a special thing. It doesn't matter much whether it's expensive, pretty, or even playable—it trains you. I wrote my first song on that guitar in my twelfth year, eventually playing it to a captive audience from the backseat of our car. I remember my mother turning and staring at me, wondering what had happened to the child she thought she was raising.

We did everything wrong. I faithfully polished it with cheap lemon oil once a month—everywhere. Fretboard, pickguard, if you were attached to my guitar you got polished. When it buzzed, I'd fold over a cardboard match-cover and stick it under the string, right up at the nut; that always worked. I took apart the tuning machines and cleaned them periodically, squirting them with WD-40 to keep them moving.

When a waitress dropped a tray on it, we had no idea where to go for repairs in East Orange, New Jersey, so my father just asked around for a good instrumental woodworker. A violin-maker in Newark rebuilt the top, reglued the braces, and installed a larger, heavier bridge plate. Having no idea how to take care of a valuable instrument, we went on instinct and *Mechanic's Weekly*. In return, The Guitar played, and played, and played.

At thirteen, I learned to write a lead sheet with it, sent the song into *Broadside* magazine, and was invited to play at the Village Gate. The Guitar and I got a standing ovation; we were on our way.

One day another performer mentioned that it was a Martin D-18, from 1937, the "pre-war years." He explained that the best wood came from then, and the best dreadnaughts. When I got home I said, "Dad! Dad! This is a Martin guitar!" He shrugged. "Yep, honey, it's a guitar. I knew that." I'd read about Martins somewhere, but it had never occurred to me that Dad's beat-up old instrument could have been *made* by anyone. It just *was*.

It became My Guitar when my father gave it to me for my sixteenth birthday. By then, my guitar and I had recorded two albums together, met Leonard Bernstein, been on *The Tonight Show*, and done concerts from coast to coast. We'd lived through my first hit, "Society's Child," getting spit on and booed off the stage by crowds chanting "Nigger lover!" We'd earned each other.

We survived being called has-beens a few hitless years later, and we wrote "Jesse" two years after that. Through the dark times, one of us, at least, had remained universally admired. Vinnie Bell, legendary New York studio musician, had offered me $5,000 for it—in 1966! Artists like Jimi Hendrix would greet me and say, "How's The Guitar doing, man? What a sweetheart!"

It was an extraordinary instrument, a 1937 D-18 that somehow, through a combination of wood, break-in, temperature, humidity, and just plain love, wound up being the best acoustic guitar any of them had ever heard. Reverend Gary Davis would beg to borrow it at folk festivals; other artists kept offering me money.

Why? It had the best bass tone I'd ever heard on a guitar, bar none. And, unusual in a guitar from that era, it sounded as good picked as strummed, flat-picked as frailed. I moved to Los Angeles in 1972 and took her with me (somehow, over the years, she'd become "her"—my closest confidante, dearest companion), hoping the more temperate climate would be good for my aging friend. One day I came back from a morning at the beach to find my apartment burglarized—and although clothing had been flung from the drawers and the place was a mess, all my credit cards and jewelry were left where they'd been. The only things missing were a rented television and my two guitars. Ironically, I'd bought a Gallagher just months earlier, having decided the road was too dangerous for my Martin.

I called the police; they were pessimistic, saying a large ring specializing in stolen guitars had been operating in L.A. for months. I called Martin Guitars, registering it as stolen. I canvassed the apartment complex. I telephoned every pawn shop in the Los Angeles area, offering a reward for any scrap of information. Then I sat, dulled by fatigue and pain, waiting and hoping.

The phone rang two days later; a young man had pawned my Gallagher, demanding exactly what it was worth "like he knew what he was doing." He'd used his draft card for ID. A few days later, the police picked him up.

I went to court and testified that I hadn't given him permission to borrow My Guitar. The detectives (knowing he already had a thirteen-page rap sheet) threatened him, trying to break the ring. And although it was illegal, I desperately offered him a $2,000 reward if he'd just bring it back, no questions asked.

In the end, he chose to do three to five years of hard time rather than reveal anything.

That was the end of that. I mourned for years—twenty-six of them, to be exact. Nothing in my life—not breakups, not the death of beloved friends and family, not the loss of every dime I had in 1986—nothing affected me more deeply. You may think that's crazy, but then again, maybe you've never owned a guitar like this one.

I became afraid to be attached—to anything. When a former accountant failed to pay taxes on my behalf and the IRS stripped me of everything down to my pride, it was relatively easy to sell what remained. My friends thought I was in shock, not caring about the things I lost that year: the Vega Tubaphone No.1 banjo, the Lloyd Baggs guitar, the house and studio and clothes and furniture. But nothing mattered after my Martin. Things were just things; everything that wasn't replaceable could be lived without. The only regret I had was parting with my Bösendorfer piano, and my heart was salved knowing it provided enough money to care for myself and my mother for six long months.

Yet somewhere in the back of my head, a small part of me clung to hope. "If she ever comes back…" I would think, "everything will be all right." When I began recording again, I put a note on each album: *Missing since 1972, Martin D-18 serial #67053. Reward for return; no questions asked.* I meant it.

I hoped someone kind had bought her, someone who played her frequently and treated her well. I hoped they bought her not knowing she was stolen. I hoped she wasn't living overseas. I hoped.

Years passed. I slowly regained my financial footing, bought a home, began a relationship that's still going strong. I began to feel like the hard times were over at last. Oh, I'd never be able to afford a Bösendorfer again, but I had guitars now, and heat in the winter again. And I'd held on to two baby Martins through the worst of it, thinking that if anyone ever returned mine (unaffordable to me at today's prices), maybe I'd be able to swap for it.

My partner graduated from law school this year, and to celebrate we took a vacation in Provincetown, Massachusetts. Over her strenuous objections, I brought my laptop with me. One day I was scanning my new mail and noticed something from a stranger. Now, I get e-mail from strangers all the time, but most of it does not have RE: YOUR D-18 in the header.

I read it with growing excitement. Eric Schoenberg, owner of a guitar shop in Tiburon, California, was telling me he had a client who had my guitar. Did I want the client's phone number?

I wrote back immediately, saying yes, then gave full rein to paranoia. Could someone have replaced the serial number on a Martin, hoping to claim a reward? For that matter, how much of a reward would they want? What were my rights under the law, and what were my ethical and moral obligations?

I contacted everyone I knew, from Stanley Jay of Mandolin Brothers to master guitarist Preston Reed. *Do you know this guy Schoenberg?* I asked. *Is he reputable? Would he lie to me, or participate in a coverup? And Geoff Grace, the fellow who says he has my guitar— does anyone know him?*

The answers flew back. Eric Schoenberg was highly respected by one and all, with an impeccable reputation. It was impossible to replace an old Martin serial number. And legally, since I'd filed a police report, the stolen property was mine. All I would owe Geoff was whatever he'd spent on maintenance and repairs.

A day later, heart in mouth, I called Geoff Grace. *He's not home, this is his mother.* Ah, he had a mother. That was already good. She lived with him, or spent time there—even better. She didn't sound like a con artist; she knew about the guitar. I sat in an agony, waiting. Hours later I was still waiting, having completely forgotten the time difference between East and West Coasts. Pat sat with me in silence.

Suddenly tears began pouring down my face. I couldn't speak, couldn't explain myself. It was as though a twenty-six-year-old dam had burst, throwing the debris of all those hopeless years out of my heart and into the open air.

When I finally became capable of speech, I spoke through my hiccups. "If it is her...if it is my Martin...then I've come full circle, finally. I'll get back the only material thing that ever mattered to me...all those years paying off the IRS, paying off the ex-husbands' debts, paying off other people's mistakes and meanness—all those years of waiting will finally be over. I can be myself again, if she comes back."

Make no mistake—I am not a fetishist. I don't cling to objects for luck, or believe my life is over without them. Yet when my Martin was stolen, it left a hole in me that nothing could replace—a big, dead spot where no life grew.

The phone rang, and I met Geoff. He told me he'd bought the guitar in 1972 from a shop in Berkeley. It was pretty beat up and someone had done a bad lacquer job on the back, so he got it for only $650. He'd had the neck reset and a couple of other things fixed, but never touched the body or frets. Oddly enough, the same guitar was stolen from *his* home in Sausalito in 1976, which is why he'd memorized the serial number. The guitar had been with him all this time; although he bought and sold instruments regularly, he'd hung on to her because "it's the best D-18 I've ever heard."

He'd read an interview with me in *Vintage Guitar* magazine by Steve Stone, praising my playing and mentioning at the end that I was still looking for my Martin. "It took me fifteen seconds to realize that was *my* Martin you were looking for," he told me. And, amazingly enough, he immediately decided to give it back. "I called two friends in the Bay Area with big mouths and told them, just to keep myself honest," he said. "I figured after that, there'd be no turning back." He then called Eric Schoenberg, knowing Eric could contact me through e-mail. The rest was history.

Now, the moment of truth. What did he want? What, in his estimation, was the guitar worth?

I won't say we fenced; he quoted a figure I couldn't afford, then thought about it and said that was for insurance purposes—the real value was half that. Even half was too much for me.

"Well, since I did file a police report, isn't it mine anyway?" I asked.

He thought about that and said yes, he supposed so. He thought some more, then said, "Hell, I don't want to keep someone else's guitar! Just tell me where to ship it—it's yours."

I couldn't do that; this man had loved my Martin as long as I had, even longer. I suggested we try a trade: he could ship it to me at my expense, and I would ship him my two small Martins, a turn-of-the-century 0-28 and a 1924 0-42. He could have whichever he liked, and the Mark Leaf case to go with it. Geoff agreed.

I arrived home and raced to the package. There she was. I pulled out the guitar and began to cry again. It was her, just as I remembered. I hugged her to myself, not daring to play just yet, only daring to remember. My partner stood, smiling, as I babbled.

"See, Pat, here's where I learned to flat-pick!"

"Oh," she wondered, "I thought you flat-picked *over* the hole, not making gouges near the fretboard."

"Sure, when you know how..." I mumbled.

"It looks awfully...old," Pat said, "kind of worn."

"Like we're not?" I fiercely answered, clutching the Martin to me. Then I burst into tears yet again, stroking the fretboard, afraid to play her. What if she didn't sound the same? The lost fish is always biggest in memory. What if she wasn't special, wasn't extraordinary? What if I'd spent the last twenty-six years mourning nothing more than an imaginary ideal?

I hit the first chord and started grinning like a fool; she sounded just like I remembered. I tuned the E down to a low D and hit a second chord. It rang forever. I pressed my ear against her side to hear the aftertones, the subtones, all the little nuances I'd missed, these long and lonely years. Everything was there. Everything was stunning. Everything was beautiful.

We were finally home.

Geoff ended up taking the small Martin I preferred, but as Pat said, "If he hadn't taken the one you liked best, what kind of sacrifice would it have been on your part? You can't get something for nothing, you know." And when I finally met Geoff and Eric a few months ago, I found myself speechless. How do you thank someone for giving back your dreams? How do you thank someone for filling a hole in your heart? Where do you find the words to explain, to make him understand that he's healed you?

The bottom line is, you can't. You can only hope he understands a small part of the gift he's given you—how it made up for every petty moment in your life; how it erased all the bad memories and left only the good. How you know now, in every fiber of your being, that in this world righteous men still walk, and you're fortunate enough to have encountered one.

Janis Ian

Born April 7, 1951, Janis Ian burst on the scene at age fifteen with her controversial saga of interracial love, "Society's Child." Self-penned and -arranged, it topped the charts and created a storm of discussion. Her debut album, 1967's Janis Ian, *garnered her the first of her nine Grammy nominations to date. Since then, there have been seventeen albums.*

Ian achieved a new level of popularity in the 1970s with her trio of masterpieces, Stars *(1973),* Between the Lines *(1975), and* Aftertones *(1976). Her song "Jesse" became a pop standard after Roberta Flack topped the charts with it. "Everyone thought 'Society's Child' was a fluke, and I was a has-been at eighteen," says Ian. "'Jesse' proved I was a real writer." Two years later, "At Seventeen" sold over a million copies and earned Ian her first two Grammy Awards.*

She entered the 1980s with the international disco hit "Fly Too High," a song featured on the sound track of the Jodie Foster movie Foxes. *This was one of several film-music ventures, and her songs have been featured on television shows as diverse as* The Simpsons *and* General Hospital. *She has also studied acting, directing, scoring, and ballet.*

But Janis Ian is truly a "musician's musician." Her songs have been recorded by Stan Getz, Bette Midler, Glen Campbell, Cher, Etta James, and many others. In 1986 she began working steadily with other writers in Nashville, Tennessee; in 1988 she officially made Nashville her home, and lives there still.

Her most recent release, god & the fbi, *marks her seventeenth album. "Always my lucky number," says Ian. You can visit her Web site at www.janisian.com.*

The River

Tim Putnam

And those were the last words he said, poor old Davies. An echo slaps the walls of the canyon and wanders off across the forest. I dig a grave for him a little bit in from the river. I know he always liked the sound of water.

After he's covered properly, I pitch a cross at the head of the grave. I cry a little and then Horse and I ride back toward town, thinking about the whole thing.

Davies and I grew up together in Dublin, California. When we were little we used to come up to this very river and fish for trout. That's how come I know he liked the sound. He was always a better fisherman than I was, but there wasn't a man closer than three states who could out-hunt me. Ladies and whores all say I can smell better than a pack of dogs and out-smart any four-legged creature that has the bad judgment to be upwind of me when my stomach rumbles.

So anyways, I grew up in Dublin and stayed around these parts for most of my life. Truth be told, I've got kind of a wanderin' spirit, so I wander right out of town on occasion, and on one occasion I moseyed upon Horse, here. He was moseyin', too, and I knew right then that we were gonna get along just fine. There was some poor old man layin' against the rocks with three bullet holes in his chest, so I figured it was my duty to take Horse and give him a new home.

When I rode back into town all the ladies and whores were admiring Horse and me, so the first place I stopped was the old saloon. In Dublin, everything's old, like it's been here since the dawn of time, like the Lord God Almighty Himself said, "Let there be light. And let there be Dublin, California. And the saloon, and the hotel, and the whole bit." I pushed the doors open and they squeaked, announcin' my entrance to the whole rowdy pack of 'em. There was a poker game going on when I walked in, and Stan the Piano-man playing the upright, and Earl the bartender serving the usual suspects surroundin' the bar.

Speakin' of ladies and whores, well, that's where Sarah Appleton comes in. Sarah Appleton was a lady *and* a whore. That's what I loved about her. She was always nice and pretty and real concerned with everybody in Dublin, but hoowhee— she can be a handful, too, if ya get what I'm saying. She stood at the top of the stairs wearing that purple dress that I just couldn't wait to get off of her and lookin' at me with that certain glint in her eye. After we made sweaty love in one of the rooms upstairs, I decided I should probably be joinin' that poker game that was going on downstairs. I wandered down the stairs, strappin' on my suspenders and slickin' my hair back.

At the table were Montgomery, Murray, Fallon, Joyce, and poor old Davies.

"Fancy meeting you boys here," I said as I smiled wide and kindly. They didn't look real happy to see me.

"Well if it ain't the Amador Valley Asshole."

"Easy, Joyce." I suppose my reputation in these parts is questionable, at best. Dublin's a nice community after all, with laws and regulations and a good dose of decorum. But hell, what man can control hisself all the time? So what if I happen to carry a few extra aces up my sleeves?

Well, by now I guess you're starting to put this all together. Yes, I cheated, Lord forgive me. And yes, I took the entire pile from each one of those poor critters. It was a nice cleanup, if I do say so myself. But I got a little bit sloppy as I was walkin' out of the saloon. I turned to give a final wave to Sarah Appleton, and when I did, three aces went gliding through the air. Well, them boys at the poker table didn't much like that, and me, being smarter than most, knew that it was time to scoot. So I jumped on Horse and rode like blazes out of town. I knew in my heart it would be the last time I would see Sarah Appleton, and the saloon, and Dublin herself. I felt like crying, and hell, I might have shed a tear.

I rode fast into the forest, like I've done many times, but not under circumstances like these. I knew this was a hunt and I smiled real wide 'cause ain't a man in three states who can hunt like me. Night sneaked up on me so I tied Horse to a tree and laid down by the river. The wind kind of whispered me to sleep.

I heard the click and I knew it was Davies's pistol aimed right at my temple.

"Get up, Virgil." I hate it when people use my first name.

"You know I hate it when people use my first name."

"I said get up." He pulled his other pistol up and locked the hammer back. Somethin' about pistols bein' cocked that's soothing like rain to me.

I stood.

It was morning. The forest was quiet. The wind was still.

"You didn't come up here alone, did you, Davies?" He got real nervous when I said that.

"You just stay put, Virgil."

Well, goddammit, that was it. I had my gun turned on him in the flutter of a hummingbird's wing. He hesitated, and in that hesitation I shot his hand. The gun fell to the ground and hit the dirt with a heavy thud.

Davies fell to his knees clutching his bad hand with his good one. He looked pathetic, not at all like he did when we used to fish down here. It breaks my heart to see a crippled man, just like Horse's old owner.

"You smell that?" I asked. Davies was a bit preoccupied. "That there is the smell of burnt gunpowder. It almost brings a tear to my eye, the way it lingers for a bit and blows away. Hell, I guess I live to smell it."

Davies had stopped his whimpering. He was calm now, but breathing heavy. I walked over and put the mouth of my gun between Davies's eyes. He started breathing heavier if you can believe it. And he looked cross-eyed. It was funny.

Neither one of us said anything for a while. It was all just too perfect with forest, the leaves, and the river. I almost shed a tear, but it wouldn't have been appropriate. I just looked at Davies for a long time, cocking back the hammer on my gun. After a while Davies spoke.

"Hurry up and shoot me, you son of a bitch."

And those were the last words he said.

Tim Putnam

Tim Putnam was born and grew up in Missouri before attending Mercersburg Academy in Pennsylvania. He moved to Nashville, Tennessee, in 1994 to attend Belmont University and landed his first cut, a cowrite with pop songster Ty Lacy, in 1995. In the years that followed, Putnam had a string of cuts, including songs with major recording artists and on the WB Network's sound-track-heavy hit show Felicity. *His poetry has been published in the* Belmont Literary Journal.

Currently he is a partner with the on-line entertainment-marketing company Music City Networks, and he cofounded Earnote, a music production house, with Scotch and Mark Ralston. Through the years he has continued to write short stories, screenplays, poetry, and, of course, songs.

He lives in Franklin, Tennessee, with his wife, Julie, and their dog, Ivy. You can visit his Web site at www.timputnam .com.

Lucky Boy

Klem Hayes

I don't think I'll ever get used to this smell. Pine-Sol, tapioca, and tapioca farts (with a hint of pine). It'd be nice if we didn't have to suffer through the same recycled Muzak day after day. I guess they figure no one will ever notice. Currently my favorite track is "Patience" by Guns N' Roses. It plays every morning during bingo. Kick ass!

Most weeks we get a group of visitors/onlookers stopping in to pay their respects. Cub Scouts are a favorite. They sing the national anthem or do a halfhearted recitation of the Pledge of Allegiance. I *think* that's what they're doing, anyway. They mumble in unison with a junior military salute staring past the old Stars and Stripes at some kid's mom holding a plate of frosted cookies. None of the kids ever makes it to the end. Sometimes I like to yell at them—nothing mean spirited, just crazy deaf old man yellin'. I'll ask them if their intentions toward my daughter are pure, "'cause dammit, sonnyboy, she's been hurt before!" I'll bark out impossible commands: "Get that dog out of my pool." Or I tell them to help themselves to a nonexistent bowl of lemon candies. Then I beg them, "Please lower your voices."

I like to think I'm their favorite.

My golden years started prematurely here at the Happy Trails Life Center. Arriving at all of forty-five years old, I was a pretty hot young item—especially among the octogenarian widows. I remember how they ogled me as I rolled into the dining hall that first day, taking an extra hit of oxygen and catcalling, "Fresssshhhh Fish!" I had a particular fondness for several dressed in bright floral muumuus with teeth that I swear they carved themselves. But my leering made them uncomfortable and they quickly backed off. The first couple of weeks I either kept to myself or hung around a defrocked priest who played low-stakes bridge. (To this day, I don't know the first thing about the game, but I won more times than I lost. I got in the habit of gathering the winnings before he could figure out who had played what cards.) He had former parishioners visit regularly who would sneak him small bottles of Jack Daniel's and blather on and on about how he was wrongly accused. When I could, I sat in on these private visits offering an affirming head-nod or a well-placed "Oh yes," biding my time until the free booze handout.

Over time I became content with my new surroundings. Subsidized long-term care for the indigent and infirmed was, quite truthfully, a homecoming of sorts.

My mother died the day I was born. I was her sixth child, her only son. The labor was unusually difficult and the doctors initially declared me a stillbirth. When I started breathing on my own they upgraded my prognosis to "likely blind with mild to severe retardation." They were mostly wrong again. My mom wasn't nearly as fortunate. On her deathbed she told the hospital minister that her new son was to be named Lucky, "after his father." Problem with that was that her husband was named Dennis. When the new proud papa took one look at me and my birth certificate, he decided he would go back home to his five legitimate daughters and call it a life. Word has it that he didn't go to Mom's funeral, and I never saw him again.

As it turned out, having the words "blind" and "retarded" on my permanent record wasn't such a bad thing. The state bureaucrats, having never been much for details, wouldn't let the fact that I was of sound mind and body cloud their judgment. They placed me in a host of special schools and homes that would have otherwise been off limits. And I thrived—sort of. Expectations were low, and I didn't disappoint.

When I was seventeen I found my father, Lucky. Like me, he was in the care of the state. But he was to remain there for two lifetimes plus fifty years. During our brief visit, he told me that he had outgrown the name Lucky and was now known by his God-given name, Lance. "Lucky," he explained, was simply a nickname he was forced to adopt during an earlier stint in jail by his then cell mate, Matador. As I left him that day, I couldn't help but wonder about the even more unfortunate turns my life might have taken if I'd been merely named Lance.

During my twenties I attended every twelve-step meeting I could find. My appetite for these groups was insatiable. At one memorable gathering, a sad sack offered sobbing testimonial recalling the entirety of his life as an "uninterrupted string of failures." I was stunned and jealous. He and I could have been carved from the same foul lump of clay, but he had already written the final sentence of his final chapter. Most impressive was that he couldn't get off his ass to do anything worthwhile but had found the time and energy to sum up his miserable life in a very profound, pointed manner. Not to be outpaced, I started trying to imagine how my headstone might read. For a long time I clung to the phrase "Swing and a Miss." I was never much of a baseball fan, but I liked the metaphor. And I liked that people who passed by my grave might think I was a sporty type. But as that slogan simmered over the years I realized that I had generously overstated my role in the game of life. Truthfully, a more accurate but cumbersome description was that I stood "Shaking at the Plate with My Eyes Closed."

To fail required some effort; an attempt made. That was further than I ever reached.

I nearly found my stride when I turned thirty. The local chamber of commerce published a bimonthly newspaper and was looking to publicize unusual services in the area. I submitted a fuzzy picture of some unknown balloon artist with one of his elaborate twisted creations. I called it "The Excitable Pup" (because it looked like a dog with an erection), and claimed it as my own. "My life's work has been displayed at the Louvre and I've entertained at the Vatican," I lied. They printed every bit of it and ranked me third in the category behind a nun who could walk on her hands and a clown college graduate. I was never hired.

I spent most of my waking hours in the public library. Nights I slept beside a Catholic church. As much as I could, I avoided other people. I wandered an upscale suburb that operated a food pantry providing me with groceries twice a week. Everything I owned—two can openers, a bottle of Listerine, and a garbage-bag poncho—I carried in a small red cooler. I tucked my hair up under a sombrero that at one time had the word *Muchacho* stitched across the front but now just read *chachi*. If anyone asked, I told them it was a gift from Scott Baio.

On the day of my forty-fourth birthday the woman who ran the food pantry told me that they were offering a free "spa day" for the community. For families with real needs that meant kids would get back-to-school flat tops or moms might get a shampoo, a cut, and a manicure. For me, it was just time to get cleaned up.

I sat on a folding chair in the basement of the village hall annex. A burly, cleanshaven barber with tattoos up and down both arms and visible above his collar approached. Without saying a word, he tied an apron around my neck and began cutting my hair. Gnarled ropes fell to the floor and I found myself drifting off to sleep listening to the gentle buzz of the electric trimmer. In a dream I was riding a small horse around the ledge of a skyscraper. As the horse stumbled, I jerked my head back and was awakened when the barber cut off the top of my right ear. It bled. Bad. Never apologizing and visibly annoyed, he dabbed it with some tissue and continued my spa day. I got a look at myself in the full-length mirror that was leaned against a wall. Other than the bleeding and the missing piece of ear, I actually looked pretty good. I stood up before he could shave my face, grabbed my cooler and sombrero, and walked out humming "Happy Birthday."

Within a few days I was feeling sick. My head hurt. I was shaking, freezing and sweating. My ear was clearly infected and too sore to touch. I had to stop wearing my brim and eventually misplaced it. Too weak to make the one-block walk to the library, I spent my days sleeping. One hot afternoon the police roused me from my spot next to the church. Paramedics arrived and I was loaded into an ambulance for a casual ride to the county hospital. They never turned on the siren, and I'm certain that on the way they stopped at a McDonald's drive-through.

Back in the care of the county's finest, I was diagnosed with a severe staphylococcus infection. I imagined my updated medical records now read, "Likely blind, with mild to severe retardation, and a life-threatening staph infection brought on by a bad haircut." They kept the lights on in the big noisy room, but I slept a lot. I couldn't stay awake. One day I started crying and didn't stop. I wanted to get up, find my cooler, and walk out the door, but my legs wouldn't respond.

Nearly eleven months after my arrival, I left the hospital the same way I came in. The paramedics paused for a cigarette before they rolled my wheelchair into the back of the ambulance and I smiled when I caught a glimpse of my reflection in the hospital door. I was quite the vision with my black terry-cloth slippers, my Adidas T-shirt, and my new gray running suit. It'd be almost forgivable to think I could pop right out of that chair and take my shiny bald head for a power walk. Exhaling one last breath of smoke, the driver crushed his cigarette and told me to hold on tight. "We're taking you home."

Around here, they incorporate some not-so-subtle ways of letting us know that it's time for bed. The lights in the hall go dark, the attendants stop responding to our calls, and the last strains of the Lynyrd Skynyrd joyride "Ooh That Smell" close out the Muzak track.

<hr>

Klem Hayes

A veteran bass player and songwriter who divides his time between Nashville and Chicago, Klem's music has been performed on radio and television and in theater, music videos, and motion pictures. Over the years, Klem has also lent his talents to live performances and recordings by all types of recording artists— the superstars, the has-beens, and the wanna-bes.

Mr. Hayes relishes his time at home with his two handsome sons, his ravishing bride, and the family's two dogs.

Cheeseburger Boogie

Bob DiPiero

Maybe it was the grill. The thousands of them that had gone before, leaving greasy footprints on the hands of time. Maybe it was the meat. Some ultimate juju concoction that defied those who would try to unlock its secrets. It's possible it could have been the bun. That toasting on said sacred grill that put the whole deal over the top. Onions? Yes, but that was too obvious. Way too obvious. They didn't even use Heinz ketchup. The quintessential Fuck You.

Finally, maybe it was the place. Jesus Jones had started out in the late sixties as some sort of Southern-fried hippie hangout. An oasis of insane sanity on the social desert that was Nashville, Tennessee, in the dying days of the sixties/seventies. If you had long hair back then, you couldn't even get served at the local Pancake House. Segregation still a foregone conclusion. Hell lurking just around the corner. Church of Christ the only sure shot to Heaven. Baptist a slippery slope to damnation. Speaking in tongues, snake handling, and tithing sure to get you an inside track to the pearly gates. Jesus Jones was a loose buckle on the Bible belt. You could get cold Budweiser inside, and hot sex in the parking lot when Vanderbilt was in session and all those impossibly blond coeds were trying so hard to get back at their Type A uncaring daddies and their hopelessly alcoholic, jealous mommies.

Unfortunately, Jesus Jones had lost its counterculture cachet through the years and had become "just another beer joint." Owners came and went. Neon beer signs went up and came down. But one thing had remained the same. One thing could not be vanquished. One thing had a life of its own and lives on to this day: THE CHEESEBURGER.

The beer remained reasonably cold. The parking lot sex had been mostly quashed by that nasty little party favor AIDS, but THE CHEESEBURGER ruled. Lived on and thrived. College profs, locals from the neighborhood, lawyers, losers, winners, retirees—they all came to pay their respects and receive communion at the wobbly chipped tables that adorned Jesus Jones. Another legion of pilgrims were the long motley line of singers, songwriters, musicians, wanna-bes, has-beens, never-weres, and hillbilly millionaires that lived, worked, lied, and died on and around that inbred clump of streets near downtown Nashville called Music Row.

He'd first had one in the late seventies. An A&R intern from the label had brought him to Jesus Jones after a concert. While he was performing in town he wanted to score some blow. Maybe a blowjob, if it wasn't too much work. While he was waiting to score he'd gotten hungry. He always got hungry after a gig. Hungry for food. Hungry for sex. Hungry for drugs. Hungry. Just hungry. It was the first real-by-God rock 'n' roll tour he'd ever been on. He had become a genuine badass electric guitar gunslinger. "The best in my price range," he used to joke.

Through the years he'd forgotten about what kind of drug he had scored, or the face of the English lit. major that buried herself drunkenly in his lap, but he'd never forgotten that Cheeseburger.

2:03 P.M.: Owen Love had been up for at least two hours already. 2002 and Owen Love: those two things did not go together. A cosmic oxymoron. In Owen's mind it was still somewhere in the late seventies/early eighties and he was still twenty-six. Learjets? Owen had been there, drinking Dom and snorting cocaine off some top-shelf titties. Big Tours? The biggest. Owen had been there making whatever flavor-of-the-month star look like he, she, "it" was actually that good. "Keep 'em laughing and wear cool clothes." That was Owen's mantra. Mr. Country Savior or Little Miss Diva really didn't have a clue just how good Owen was. But that was okay. As long as he got the gig.

That was the trouble right now. Owen didn't have the gig. For the first time in a long time, Owen Love didn't have a paying job as a musician. As a matter of fact, his last gig had sucked pretty hard. There was no Learjet involved. No brand-new Prevost tour bus with a bunk directly over the rear wheel to call home. Just a very late model Silver Eagle that used to belong to some over-the-hill Rock Star and was now being leased by a bipolar bulimic country chick singer who hadn't had a hit in five years. Make that seven and counting. The honky-tonks, hat bars, and cinder-block skull orchards he had played on his way up he was now playing again. Not a good sign. Definitely not a good sign. That's why he had come to Jesus Jones. That's why he had taken up his sentry post at the bar.

Owen's shaggy black hair hung unkempt around his puffy oval face. The last ten years had put on an unwelcome twenty pounds, mostly around his middle. A rocker with a beer gut. Bad form. Bad for business. He could still get layed but no longer by the Diva and lately not even the background singer.

Viagra gave him a headache and made him see everything with a blue halo around it. Lately he had pretty much lost interest anyway.

Owen wore his trademark black jeans, blue denim work shirt, and Harley boots. He'd given up wearing shades sometime back in the nineties. If he wasn't cool enough by now, Owen thought, he was fucked. He regarded his reflection in the mirror behind the bar. Rough. Still some handsome left, but he could almost see it sweating out of his skin. One too many tequila shots backstage. One too many bumps from the A&R guy who was protecting his investment and his own ass. Like James Brown said, payback was a Mother Fucker. The time had come and Owen knew it. He needed intercession. He needed healing. He had come for most Holy Communion. Owen Love had come to Jesus Jones for THE CHEESEBURGER.

When Owen had gotten divorced from his first wife, Nikki, he holed up in Jesus Jones for three straight days and nights. Living on cigarettes, Stolichnaya lemon-flavored vodka, and the occasional C.B. Up until Katie, he had been batting a thousand. If a girl was dysfunctional, delusional, damaged, or any combination thereof, she would end up in Owen's bed and entangled in his showbiz life. Sometimes she would even end up married to Owen Love. Nikki was one of those girls. One of a kind of a kind. Thank God He didn't make any more of those. One day Rachel Agnes Felder woke up and became Nikki. Just Nikki. She claimed that her style was somewhere between Sheryl Crow and Dolly Parton, whatever the hell that meant. Owen knew better than to argue taste or style with Rachel/Nikki. A year into their marriage, she'd developed this mysterious Euro Trash accent. It freaked Owen out because Rachel/Nikki had been born and raised in Morgantown, West Virginia. She'd also developed a taste for a German Chemicals rep named Claus she had met while Owen had been out on the road for a six-week tour of the West Coast and Canada. Owen had come directly to Jesus Jones from divorce court. Even though that was years ago, give or take a few thousand brain cells, Owen remembered exactly what he had ordered.

"Hey man, gimme two cheeseburgers and some burnt fries. Oh yeah. And lemme have a Fresca and a Darvon."

Owen used laughter like a shield. He always found it amazing that Charlie Chaplin had written the song "Smile." The ultimate armor. When Owen had been a theory and harmony student at Juilliard he had analyzed Chaplin's song three ways: harmonically, lyrically, and spiritually. It was that last part that had really fucked up his theory and harmony prof.

"Ya know what I think, Professor Brite? I think you gave me a C-minus because you're threatened by me."

"Mr. Love, certainly you don't—"

"You just couldn't give me an F. But you found something worse, didn't you? You gave me a C-minus, you pretentious little—"

"Now, Owen, I can certainly understand your—"

"It never entered your mind that just because Chaplin, or for that matter Mozart or Hank Williams, were geniuses they could also be totally spiritually bankrupt. You don't wanna believe it and you are envious of the fact that you can't go there and I can. I know the truth! You don't and you can't deal with it!"

That was the day Owen quit Juilliard, quit studying theory and harmony. That was the day Owen stopped playing classical piano, traded his Martin 0018 for a '56 Tele and a Vox AC-30, kept his mouth shut, and went on the road.

2:53 P.M.: In L.A. there's a place that claims to have the world's best cheeseburger. Actually, there are dozens of them there. First of all, show-biz people in L.A. don't eat cheeseburgers. They eat each other. At least that was Owen's truth at the moment. The charismatic savants will pose by a burger, but they definitely don't swallow. Point number two: The claim is utter bullshit. Courtney Love being seen on *E! News Weekend* riding her Harley to the best cheeseburger in the world is Antichrist advertisement. He might have to work with them, but enough is enough. *Anyway,* Owen thought, *the last meat she had in her mouth definitely wasn't a cheeseburger.*

What sat in front of Owen was the genuine article. The Holy Grail. Sitting there on a virginal white mini platter, nestled among a perfect nest of overdone fries. Super-sour pickle chips anointing the top. There sat THE CHEESEBURGER. Owen had found through the years of coming to Jesus Jones that it almost didn't matter how he dressed his burger. If he was in a ketchup mood he was known to go through half a bottle per burger-and-fry unit. Sometimes a white trash burger was in order. Major mayonnaise followed by ketchup, mustard, and a goodly shot of Texas Pete hot sauce. Sometimes the way they did it in certain parts of Texas was the way to go. Double mustard. And not that bullshit fancy kind. Plain bright yellow mustard. The color yellow not found in nature.

Ultimately Owen found it was all about the burger. Kinda like God's word. It wasn't about speaking in tongues, not eating meat on Friday, fasting, going to church on Wednesday, crawling on your knees to some plaster saint, sitting shiva, or any hundreds of the forms of baptism that existed. No. It was all about communing directly with your higher power. And right now God and Owen were sharing a cheeseburger.

3:05 P.M.: The door to Jesus Jones lurched open. There in the doorway, blocking almost every bit of late-afternoon Nashville light, stood, somewhat tentatively, J. C. Doubletree. All five foot seven, three hundred and thirteen pounds of him. One of Nashville's legendary songwriters. Just ask him.

"OWEN-BY-GOD-LOVE!!!!!!! Szat you? Shit! I been missin' you! Hey! Esther! Whut color panties you wearin'? Never mind. I'll find out later. I think I'd like two cheeseburgers, double fries, and a pitcher of Bud. Just a little somethin' to hold me over till Mama puts dinner on the table. Hey man! You hear 'bout them finding a box with Jesus' brother's bones in it? Jesus' brother!? That's like bein' Frank Sinatra Jr. on steroids! Haw haw haw haw!"

Owen had grown used to the "Doubletree entrance."

"Hey, Tree. What up? You look a little crispy."

"Man! You ain't agonna believe this shit. Hey Esther, ya better gimme a bowl a chili while I wait."

"You need to slow down, J.C. You're sweatin' right through your overalls."

"Too much fun, my brutha, too much fun. Me 'n' Bumpus was writin' yesterday and we couldn't come up with shit so we decided to take a li'l break. Man! I ain't even been home yet. Momma's gonna have my ass! Anyway, me and Bumpus got higher than Hitler's gas bill, I tell ya! HAW HAW HAW!!!!!!!!!!!"

J.C. absentmindedly started pulling fries off of Owen's plate. When he reached for the last two bites of Owen's burger, Owen very deftly rapped J.C.'s kielbasa fingers with the back of his knife. J.C. hardly reacted. He just started ladling steaming hot chili into his still-conversing mouth. Owen was in awe of the way J. C. Doubletree could consume just about anything. Owen recalled coming off of the Garrisons third farewell tour a few years ago. He had spent the good part of an afternoon observing a pair of hummingbirds at his window feeder. There they were, floating in air at the little plastic-flower feeding tube, relentlessly sucking down prodigious amounts of sugar water. What had amazed Owen the most at the time was the fact that these teeny little hummingbirds were shitting while they were eating. Shitting and eating. Eating and shitting. Simultaneously. Owen thought if he were Hindu he might suspect these were rajahs reincarnated as hummingbirds to set their gluttonous cosmic balance sheet straight. By this time J.C. was into his second cheeseburger, tearing off Herculean bites. Oblivious to the fact that a righteous river of ketchupmustardmayonaisehotsauce was starting to well up in the folds of his overalls bib.

"By the way, Tree, congrats on your latest number one."

"Love, I amaze myself sometimes. I really do. Course it's my first hit in about three years, but lemme tell you, my brutha, my goal is to die unrecouped. HAW HAW HAW HAW HAW!!!!!!!!!!!!!!"

Suddenly J. C. Doubletree started coughing and hacking uncontrollably. Bits of cheeseburger went sailing through the air. The empty Bud pitcher was knocked over and landed with an unbreakable-glass thud. Owen started beating J.C. on his round blubberized back.

"Whoa back there, J.C.! Yer gonna have a stroke right here! Chill out. Here. Esther brought you some water. Drink some."

"Water! Fish fuck in water!"—gurgle . . . cough . . . cough— "Gimme a beer!"

As quick as J.C. was seized by choking, it was over.

"Well, gotta go. Momma's havin' pork chops for dinner. I got to go to my AA meeting tonight. Makes Momma proud. Guess I'll be pickin' me up another one of them white chips again. I swear, I got enough of them to have me a poker game. HAW HAW HAW! I'll check out yer panties later, Esther. By the way, how you doin', Owen?"

"Well Tree, I'll tell ya. Not so goo—"

"Well, got to go. I believe I might get me some pussy tonight. I haven't seen my dick in three days. HAW HAW HAW . . . Hey! Them are the best cheeseburgers on the planet! I believe I'm gonna write a song about 'em. 'Cheeseburger Boogie!' HAW HAW HAW HAW!"

And with that, J. C. Doubletree was gone.

Owen used to court Katie with cheeseburgers from Jesus Jones. It was better than flowers as far as Hack was concerned. Katie had acquired the name Hack from the deeply prodigious cough produced by her frequent asthma attacks. Katie always came home depressed after a visit to her asthma specialist, but a Jesus Jones cheeseburger could raise her spirits. For a while anyway. The doctor said Katie's asthma was quite dangerous and needed constant monitoring. The problem was Katie hated doctors. Ever since third grade and Dr. Kaufman, Katie hated doctors. Owen had just gotten his first cell phone. He had stopped going out much, but sometimes he just had to get out to breathe living air. Somehow the kind of amp he would be using on the next tour didn't seem to matter as much as before. The cell phone was big and clunky, but when he went out he wanted to make sure Katie could always reach him. They had a game they would play when Katie was feeling good.

"Hello?"

"Hey hotshot."

"You okay, Hack?"

"Awesome, fabulous"—cough—"never better. Baby needs something."

"What does baby need?"

"She needs it hot. She needs it now."

"You want fries with that?"

"No. Just the burger. Extra mustard. Hurry."

"Yeah? Well if you kick off before I get there, I'll never speak to you again."

"Ya know, if you ever get tired of playing music, you have a huge future in comedy."

"Mocking me, eh? Somebody's feeling better."

"Hurry up, hotshot."

Owen was so very angry at Hack for dying. He could barely forgive her. So unnecessary. So very fucking unnecessary. There she was. On the floor in the kitchen of their rented home in Sylvan Park. Lying there like some giant child's discarded Barbie doll. A look of surprise on her still-open gray-green eyes. No soul left but still the reflection of another's. A mango-colored rescue inhaler under the kitchen table. The telephone receiver lying close by.

After the funeral they all gathered at Jesus Jones. Katie's parents even came. J. C. Doubletree and his plump bank-teller wife, Carol Ann, were there, and all the girls from Katie's Pilates class, Katie's gay brother Jeremy, and another half-dozen close friends. Nikki had even threatened to come. She said she had written a song for the occasion and she wanted to premiere it at this event. J.C. had somehow convinced Nikki that a larger venue would be more respectful of her work. Once Nikki agreed, she had suddenly begged off paying her respects to Owen and showing up altogether.

Owen had ordered a cheeseburger but never took a bite. It was like he had gone deaf. Like cotton had been stuffed in his ears. And his heart. People came up to him to say their regrets and he responded, but it was automatic. He was under water. It felt like the time he and Katie had gone diving in Bonaire. Her asthma prevented her from diving, but not Owen. He'd been down a little too long and had gotten narced. He had felt queasy, a little dizzy, disoriented, and somewhat stoned. That's how Owen felt that day at Jesus Jones. Sitting there wearing his best black Manuel suit, staring at his cheeseburger and talking under water. It would be two years before he could cry. Today was the day.

J.C. had been gone about ten minutes. Owen felt it coming. Like a rainstorm in the distance. Heavy weather approaching. He could feel it in his face. An ache. A bitter taste in his mouth like some kind of metal. First an odd sort of smile and an odd laugh. Then came the tears. Big, round, salty tears. They rolled down his face and soaked his T-shirt. He did not try to hide them or wipe them away. "You Can't Stop the Rain." One of J.C.'s songs. *Well, the fat fuck was right,* Owen thought as he let two years' worth of sadness, loneliness, and regret out into the world. Regret that reached beyond Katie's casket; beyond all the missed opportunities, the blame, the resentments, Rachel/ Nikki, that lost twenty-six-year-old guitar player with a big future ahead of him. The shit. All of it. Owen sat there staring it all down. Tasting it. Finally feeling it. "So let it in and let it out," like the Beatles had said. And it felt good. Right there in Jesus Jones. It felt good.

Esther, being the consummate professional bar maid that she was, knew there were times you let your patrons alone and times when you didn't.

"You okay, Owen?"

"Ah...yes and no. Kinda sorta. Yes and no. Mostly yes, I guess."

"J.C. step on your toe?"

"Naw."

Esther wiped her small hands on the greasy bar towel as she regarded Owen Love. "Life's a bitch and then ya die."

"Oobla Dee Oobla Da."

"Some days you eat the bear and some days the bear eats you."

"You Can't Always Get What You Want."

"Oh shit, Owen. I never met anyone that can speak in song titles like you."

"Well, it could be worse. I could be a mime with Tourette's."

"What?"

"Never mind. Even I don't know what that means."

"Well then, is there anything I can do for ya, darlin'?"

Owen looked into Esther's thousand-year-old eyes. He glanced around the elegantly wasted interior of Jesus Jones. A four-second eternity passed. Then he turned back to Esther, heaved a big sigh, and said,

"Yeah. Put some money in the jukebox and gimme a CHEESEBURGER."

＞＞＜

Bob DiPiero

Originally hailing from Ohio, Bob DiPiero graduated from Youngstown State University's Dana School of Music before uprooting for Music City on Halloween night over twenty years ago. After sharpening his songwriting skills, he acquired a writer's deal with Atlantic Records.

His early writing credits include Reba McEntire's "I Can See Forever in Your Eyes" and the Oak Ridge Boys' "American Made," which received numerous awards and was used in major ad campaigns.

A two-time recipient of CMA's Triple Play Award, DiPiero has gone on to craft over thirteen number-one hits recorded by country music legends including Vince Gill, Reba McEntire, Shenandoah, George Strait, Jo Dee Messina, Martina McBride, and Faith Hill. In 2000, he was named Songwriter of the Year by Sony/ATV, Nashville.

In 1987, DiPiero established Little Big Town Music Group with Woody Bomar and Kerry O'Neil, and created American Made Music as a copublishing company. And in 1998, he founded Love Monkey Music through Sony/ATV Tree Publishing Company.

As a performer, Bob DiPiero toured with Garth Brooks, Nitty Gritty Dirt Band, and Hank Williams as part of the group Billy Hill, best known for the hit single, "Too Much Month at the End of the Money" and a rendition of the Temptations hit "I Can't Help Myself (Sugar Pie, Honey Bunch)." In recent days, DiPiero has entertained Music City locals at Nashville's infamous Bluebird Cafe. Live renditions of several DiPiero performances and unforgettable stories from the Bluebird are featured on his album Laugh. *You can visit his Web site at www.bobdipiero.com.*

A Burning Bush Will Do

Marshall Chapman

The night Ellie Greenway broke up with her boyfriend she took a chainsaw to her queen-size four-poster bed. The bed was an antique that had been in her family for generations. The chain saw belonged to Bob, a graphic designer who lived down the hall. A part of her knew there'd be hell to pay if any of the members of her family ever found out about what she had done, but she was too upset to care. Besides, it felt too good. That chain saw moved through those mahogany posts like a hot knife through butter. One, two, three, four—and then the whole canopy came crashing down on her mattress.

Bob had heard them fighting that night, and when everything had quieted down it seemed like no time at all before Ellie was standing there knocking at his door. He knew it was Ellie because he knew her knocks. She had different knocks for different things. It was well past midnight and he knew that this knock meant business.

"I need your chainsaw," she said.

Bob was taken aback. He'd known Ellie for two years now and he thought he had learned always to expect the unexpected from her, but this was new. She had never asked to borrow his chainsaw before.

"Alex and I had a fight," she added as if that was all the explanation that was needed.

Bob had never liked Alex. He thought Alex was an untrustworthy egotistical bore and couldn't for the life of him understand Ellie's attraction. He secretly hoped that she had killed Alex during their argument and now she needed his chainsaw to cut Alex's body down to manageable sizes for flushing down the toilet. That would serve him right. What an asshole! These thoughts were running through Bob's head as he moved across his living room to the chainsaw in the closet. He lifted it out of there and handed it over to Ellie.

"Thanks," she said.

Bob stood there in a daze as he watched her walk out the door. She was halfway back down the hall before he could think to ask her if she needed any help.

"Hey! Do you need any help?" He felt stupid the minute he said it.

"I'll manage," she said, and Bob knew that she would.

The chainsaw had made so much noise that Ellie thought she might get arrested or at least evicted for disturbing the peace, but neither of these things happened. What happened was nothing, and that's what made her crazy. She was standing there all alone in the most silent silence she had ever known. Without the chainsaw she began to hear herself think, and that was the last thing in the world she wanted to hear: *Now what are you going to do? Where's Alex? Is he okay? You don't care so why are you asking? Oh my God would you look at this mess! And your bed? Why, all the king's horses and all the king's men will never get that bed back like it was.* For a minute the dialogue stopped and there was only a strange noise. Ellie thought it might be the sound of her own heart breaking and that's when she knew she had to get the hell out of there. She needed noise and she needed speed, so she decided to kill two birds with one 1968 Pontiac Catalina. She decided she was going for a ride.

As soon as she was out on the interstate, Ellie reached for the radio, punching in the local college station on the far left-hand side of the dial. Gram Parsons was singing with raw emotional power:

> *In my hour of darkness*
> *In my time of need*
> *Oh Lord grant me vision*
> *Oh Lord grant me speed*

With that, she cranked up the volume as loud as it would go, then gripped the steering wheel with both hands—elbows straight—so that the vibrations of the road moved through her body like a jackhammer, shaking her down until she and the car became one moving mass of gasoline and adrenaline. Ellie pressed on harder and harder, wondering just how fast the old car would go before it blew up or something. She was about to break her old speed record of ninety-five miles an hour—a record that had been established the summer she was fourteen years old. She and Lucy Dow and Monte Pringle had taken her grandmother Danny's brand-new 1963 Cadillac up to Ocean Drive Beach for the afternoon. Danny had gone out to play bridge with some friends and wasn't due back until six o'clock that evening.

For as long as Ellie could remember, everybody had called her grandmother Danny. That was her nickname. Her real name, they joked, was Dangerous. Danny was always having wrecks on account of her poor eyesight and vodka consumption. The

South Carolina State Highway Department had tried taking her driver's license away, but she had given them so much hell that they finally gave up and left her alone. So every year she had to buy at least one new Cadillac, and every year it was the same color. Black. Danny always said there were three things in this world that should always be black: your Bible, your phone, and your Cadillac.

Meanwhile, Ellie could barely see over the steering wheel and her toes barely reached the accelerator as she, Lucy Dow, and Monte Pringle went careening down the King's Highway like a bat out of hell, trying to make it back to Pawleys Island in time for Danny's return from her bridge game. Ellie had made a choice that afternoon. Do I break the law and risk my own life and the lives of my two best friends? Or do I suffer the wrath of Danny? The answer was easy. She knew instinctively from years of good breeding that it was okay to risk your life to save face. They had made it. They had not been caught, and the excitement of the drive kept her up half the night listening to the ocean out beyond the sand dunes.

The memory of that summer got Ellie to thinking about how much simpler life was back then. Back before boys. It was the summer the Angels sang "My boyfriend's back and there's gonna be trouble, hey-la, hey-la..." Ellie thought about all the boyfriends in her life and how much trouble they had been. Not trouble for other people on her behalf, but trouble for her. Boyfriends had always been her trouble.

Now she glanced down at the lit-up speedometer where the needle was vibrating at 105 miles an hour. Ellie acknowledged this new speed record by pressing down on the horn and holding it. Then she began to scream at the top of her lungs. The radio was already going full blast, so you can imagine how it was. That '68 Pontiac should have blown up, but there was a delicate balance at play here between the wind pressure outside and noise pressure inside that actually held the car together. Later on, Ellie would come to realize that sometimes it takes a little noise and speed just to keep life from caving in on you. Life could crush you down to nothing in a second if you let it.

THEN ELLIE saw something that made her stop screaming, let go of the horn, and take her foot up off the accelerator, all at the same time. What looked like a sea of flashing blue lights was waiting about a mile up ahead on the interstate. And in the rearview mirror, there were more blue lights coming up behind. Then a funny thing happened. Ellie took in a long, deep breath and let it out real slow. A relaxed resignation settled down on her and she was not afraid. In fact, she had never felt more calm. She didn't even touch the brakes. She decided to let the Catalina just wind on down to a stop on its own. They were still winding down to the tune of about eighty miles an hour as they blew right past the flashing blue lights that'd been up ahead only seconds before. Meanwhile, the blue lights in the rearview mirror had caught up and now a patrol car was breathing down her tailpipe. Ellie turned off the radio. Then she heard a voice that sounded like it was coming through a loudspeaker. "Pull over," it said. "Pull your car over to the right. We repeat…" Ellie decided it was time to apply the brakes. She then eased the Catalina off the interstate and brought it to a complete stop.

"Lady, do you have any idea how fast you were doin' back there?"

"No, sir." Ellie's father had taught her always to be respectful when talking to officers of the law.

"We've got you on the clock doin' 103 mph."

"Yes, sir."

"You in some kind of a hurry?"

"No, sir. I'm just real upset, sir."

"You ain't been drinkin' now, have you?"

"No, sir, but I wish I had."

The patrolman ignored this last comment, asked to see her driver's license, then walked around to the back of her car, where he wrote her out one ticket for speeding and then another one for reckless driving. Reckless driving? Ellie was incensed. Sure, she'd been driving fast, but she had not been driving bad. The nerve! Ellie kept these thoughts to herself as more patrol cars began arriving on the scene. The patrolman waved them on like he had everything under control. Then he instructed Ellie to follow him to the local courthouse located about five miles off the next exit. Once off the interstate, Ellie felt like she had crossed over into the twilight zone. Here she was, following a strange man down a dark and winding road going God knows where. She began to wonder if she'd ever see civilization again. Then she saw a house by the side of the road. Then another, and another, until there were houses everywhere. In some of them, people were watching television, totally oblivious to anything outside of their own little world. And that included Ellie Greenway as she passed by in her 1968 Pontiac Catalina on this dark moonless night.

At the courthouse, Ellie learned that her bail had been set at two hundred and fifty dollars. She also learned that there would be no judge and therefore no hearing until nine o'clock the next morning. *Damn these small towns! Where the hell am I, anyway? Why can't I be in my own county where I know people? And how on God's green earth did I ever get so far away from home in such a short period of time?* Ellie entertained herself with these questions just to keep from thinking about anything else. But the time had come to make a decision. She could either call Bob to come bail her out or spend the rest of the night in jail. She had already bothered Bob once tonight and that was enough—but no, there was more to it than that. Ellie realized she wanted to go to jail. Jail would be an improvement over her life right now. She was tired of being responsible for herself and she was ready to let someone else have the job. Even if it was the Wilson County jail. "There's no one for me to call," she lied. "I'll stay here tonight." With that, she was led past a door with a sign on it that said NO GUNS BEYOND THIS POINT! Ellie read the sign and thought to herself, *I'm already going to a better place.*

But Ellie had never been to jail before and now that she was there, she began to have second thoughts about it being a better place. First of all, she was not alone. There were three other women in there with her. She was careful not to look any of them in the eye for fear she would become one of them— become a prisoner. She was not about to let that happen. She was Ellie Greenway and she would remain Ellie Greenway no matter what. But still she saw them. One had her hair slicked back in a ducktail and was wearing a black leather jacket with her thumbs hitched down in her Levi's just like Marlon Brando in *The Wild One.* On top of that, she was chain-smoking non-filter Camels, holding each one between her thumb and index finger while she huffed and puffed like she was about to blow somebody's house down. And facial hair? Ellie had never seen so much facial hair on a woman.

If that's not a lesbian, then I've never seen one, Ellie thought.

She also thought that this woman would have made a real sexy man, a man she might have been attracted to enough to start a conversation with. But no, she was a woman, and Ellie decided not to say anything to her just in case she really was a lesbian and hated her for not being one too. Another woman sat huddled up on a bench in the corner. She was young. No more than fourteen or fifteen. A steady stream of tears fell down her face as she cried silently to herself. The third woman's name was Ruby Louise. At least that was the name in gold letters hanging at the end of a gold necklace around her neck. She was leaning up against the wall by the door and had a no-nonsense seen-it-all air about her that Ellie trusted. Her expression was one of boredom and amusement with just the slightest hint of disgust.

"Damn, you'd think it was New Year's Eve the way they're bringin' 'em in tonight."

Ellie ignored this comment as she made her way over to an empty cot in the far corner of the room. She wanted to get as far away from the others as she could. As she sat there with her head resting heavy in her hands, she began focusing all of her energy inward. Harder and harder she focused, hoping to make herself invisible, but it wasn't working. Something wasn't right. It was then that she noticed the toilet seat out in the middle of the room. There was nothing fancy about it, just your basic white porcelain bowl. But then there was nothing to lend privacy or hold back the stench that was now making Ellie want to gag. And in that moment, there came forth a horrible realization. Ellie was about to die to go to the bathroom. Only there was no bathroom. Just this porcelain reminder that death might not be such a bad deal after all. As she sat there unconsciously squirming she again heard the voice of Ruby Louise.

"Honey, you want a bullet to bite on? Now why don't you just go on over there and set your ass down where you can do yourself some good. Now git!"

Ellie waited a bit before making a move. She didn't want it to look like she had heard anything anybody had said. *Oh God, this has got to be the pits! Life just can't get any lower than this,*

Ellie thought as she painfully positioned herself over the toilet seat and then proceeded to release the pressure from her lower abdomen right there in front of God, Ruby Louise, and anybody else who cared to watch. 'Course nobody was watching, or at least they pretended not to be watching, but Ellie knew God was watching and that was good enough for her. Ellie wondered if it hurt God's feelings to see her like this. Who knows? Maybe He was having a big laugh at her expense. But there was one thing she knew for sure. She and God would be having a big talk before this night was through.

When Ellie was safe back in her corner, she began to think about what-all had happened so far that night. Too much had happened too fast, and it was all swirling around in her head and making her dizzy. It was just too much to think about all at once, so the left side of her brain kicked in, trying to sort everything out and put it in some kind of order that made sense. But nothing made sense. Ellie felt like she was watching a rerun of somebody else's bad movie. Driving 103 miles an hour? Chainsawing a mahogany bed? Not just any mahogany bed, but the very one her mother had been born in? Christ on a crutch! And then there was the fight with Alex. God, that seemed like so long ago that Ellie couldn't even remember what they had been fighting about. And now here she was in jail! Hell, if they'd really known what all had happened that night, they'd have probably put her in some special jail for the dangerously insane!

"Hey mama, you look like you need a smoke."

Without looking up, Ellie knew that Marlon Brando was standing there offering one of her non-filter Camel cigarettes. Ellie hated cigarettes. But more than that, she hated the idea of talking to anybody right now. She was in no mood for small talk.

"I said, you look like you need a smoke."

"Aw, leave her alone, Darlene. She don't want to mess with you," chipped in Ruby Louise.

"Bug off, Ruby."

Normally, Ellie would have been frightened by this show of aggressiveness, but not tonight. Not this night. This was no night for normal. Ellie felt strangely protected by something bigger than herself, bigger than this jail—hell, bigger than the whole damn world itself. Maybe the law of probability was starting to stack up in her favor. I mean she'd already been through all sorts of hell tonight. So what if some biker lesbian was coming on to her. Big deal! Besides, Ellie knew how to take care of herself. Why, about five years ago she was coming out of this all-night diner in Nashville when this Cuban-looking guy came outa nowhere pointing a gun at her.

"Okay, let's have it," he demanded quickly under his breath.

"What do you mean, 'Let's have it'!" Ellie shrieked. "Let's have it? Look, if you don't stop fucking around with me, one of us is going to die and I don't care if it's me!" (Ellie had been real depressed that year.)

The man's eyes widened with disbelief as he backed away. "Okay, lady, take it easy." He then turned and scurried off muttering "Jesus!" as he slipped back into nowhere. Later on, when Ellie was reflecting back on this incident, she came up with her "crazier-than-thou" theory of survival. It went like this: If somebody thinks you're crazier than they are, chances are they won't mess with you. And now as Darlene stood there polluting her space, Ellie could feel her own energy surge as she shifted into crazier-than-thou.

"So you don't smoke? Fine, that's okay. I was just trying to be"—Darlene blew a big puff of smoke in Ellie's face—"friendly, that's all. So what are you in here for? I mean, you don't look like the kind of girl who just woke up one morning and decided she'd spend the night in jail. So what gives?"

There was a long silence as Ellie sat there motionless. She looked just like that statue by Rodin called *The Thinker*. Then, just as Darlene was beginning to think Ellie was deaf or even retarded, she heard a word that seemed to come out of nowhere.

"Homicide."

"Huh?" Darlene spun around, not sure who or what had spoken.

"I killed somebody."

The voice came from Ellie, who by now looked like she was in some kind of trance.

"No shit!" Darlene was getting excited. "How'd it happen?"

There was another long silence. Then...

"A chainsaw—it happened with a chainsaw."

A deeper silence fell over the room. Darlene turned around and looked at Ruby Louise, who gave her a look that said, *Better back off, honey. I believe we got us a live one.* Darlene took this as a warning and went on back to her corner, where she sat down and began thumbing through a biker magazine. The teenaged girl was no longer crying.

Ellie felt a lot better. She could breathe again. But this little victory brought only a moment's peace. Then she started thinking about Alex. If he'd been here, none of this would've happened. That son of a bitch! Where was he when she needed him? Then she started thinking about all the good times, like that time they drove to Memphis for the weekend right after her father had died. Alex was sweet! They'd checked into the Peabody Hotel and spent most of the weekend ordering up room service and making love. Their only outing was to the Rendezvous across the street and down an alley where they'd eaten enough ribs to sink a battleship. What a weekend. They never even made it out to Graceland. Ellie started thinking about the way Alex made love. God, he was good. He knew exactly how to touch her. It was a gift. Most men you had to tell them or show them and then there'd be a lot of fumbling around before it ever got any good. But not Alex. He knew from the very beginning. He just knew. It was too bad they couldn't spend the rest of their lives making love, 'cause everything else about their life was pure-T-hell. When they weren't fighting, Alex was storming off somewhere and Ellie would spend the next couple of days worrying herself sick. By the time he'd come back home she'd be so glad to see him that she wouldn't even ask where he'd been or who he'd been with. Besides, if she said anything there'd just be another fight and he'd be gone again. What a bind! Ellie was sick of the whole damn thing. At least this time she was the one doing the leaving. But she couldn't even do that right! Ellie felt sure that when Alex would storm off, he invariably ended up in the arms of another woman, maybe one of her best girlfriends or even her sister. She wouldn't put it past him. Now here she storms out on him for a change and where does she end up? In jail. Sometimes life just didn't seem fair. *Wait a minute!* Ellie almost said it out loud. *How can I wish Alex was here? Hell, he's the reason I'm here!* Ellie seriously began to consider that she might be losing her mind. Then her memory started coming back. She started remembering their fight. Ah, yes...drinking. That was it! That was always it. Alex had come home drunk. Drunk and still drinking. Now the irony of it all: *He's out there free as a bird and drunk out of his mind and I'm locked up in here stone-cold sober.* Ellie wanted to scream out loud, but she didn't say anything. Then finally, she began to cry. It was a good thing too, because her head really was about to explode. Maybe that's why we cry...to keep our heads from exploding. People who never cry must not let their feelings ever get to their heads. There's just not enough room in one human head for reason and emotion too, so something has to give.

As her tears subsided, Ellie's thoughts began to turn toward God or whoever it was out there in control of everything. She was ready to bargain. She promised God that she would not have any more boyfriends unless He personally instructed her to do so.

"You're gonna have to give me some sort of sign," she said. "And I don't mean the wind blowing in the trees. I can see that any old day. It's got to be something obvious. Something that'll really get my attention. Like a burning bush. Yeah, that's it. A burning bush right there in the middle of my living room. Oh God, if I came home and saw that I would know that you meant business. I'll be looking out for you, okay?"

In the silence that followed, Ellie became aware of little things...her breathing, the ticking of her wristwatch, even her own heartbeat. And as she curled up on her side, drawing her knees up to her chest, a heaviness settled down over her like a blanket.

Later on, as the first light of dawn began to soften that darkest of nights, Ellie could have sworn she heard the ocean out there somewhere.

"But the ocean is six hundred miles away," said a tired voice of reason.

"No," answered a strange and wonderful voice. "It's just out there beyond the sand dunes."

Ellie smiled in her sleep.

Marshall Chapman

Marshall Chapman was the first woman to front a rock-and-roll band, back when women weren't yet picking up electric guitars. She rose from her conservative South Carolina background to become a versatile, acclaimed, and playfully irreverent songwriter and pioneer performer. To date she has released ten critically acclaimed albums, and her songs have been recorded by a variety of artists, including Emmylou Harris, Wynonna, Jimmy Buffett, Joe Cocker, Jessi Colter, John Hiatt, Olivia Newton-John, Dion, Irma Thomas, and Ronnie Milsap.

In 1998, Marshall and songwriting pal Matraca Berg contributed fourteen songs to Good Ol' Girls, *a country musical based on the stories of Lee Smith and Jill McCorkle, which continues to play throughout the South. Marshall's first book,* Goodbye, Little Rock and Roller *(St. Martin's Press, 2003) was a 2004 SEBA Book Award finalist, and one of three finalists for the Southern Book Critics Circle Award.*

More recently, Marshall has performed across the country, developing a one-woman show called The Triumph of Rock and Roll Over Good Breeding; *written commentaries for* The Bob Edwards Show *(XM radio); and toured in support of* Mellowicious!, *her first studio album in nine years. She is currently at work on a new book called* They Came to Nashville. *You can visit her Web site at www.Tallgirl.com.*

Born and Raised in
Black and White

Don Cook

Before I headed east to pursue my destiny, I had a bliss-
fully noneventful childhood in what history books call the
Wild Horse Desert region of Texas. My hometown may best
be described as one of the many places in the world where you
truly have to live there to really like anything about it. In fact,
that may be the best definition of the concept of "hometown"
I have ever heard. One would think a place in a part of the
country with such a picturesque name would likely resemble
a Hollywood western movie set, but our little town was just a
dustier, drier version of what most little towns in America must
have been like in the early sixties.

In my memory, flawed as it is, there was but one cowboy in
our town and, ironically enough, his name was Farmer Brown.
(I am not kidding.) He was not a working cowboy, but he was,
by all accounts, a saddle and boot maker of the highest order,
so I guess technically he was sort of a Cowboy Emeritus. I used
to go to the Sunshine Café with my mom before school to have
a cake doughnut and chocolate milk, and I remember being
fascinated watching him come in every morning and drink his

coffee in what was undoubtedly the "cowboy way." He would never drink from the cup but would instead swirl the coffee into the saucer and drink out of it. My mom always said that was how he cooled it so it wouldn't burn his mouth, but I could not believe a tough guy like Farmer Brown would worry about how hot the coffee was, so I wrote it off to great style rather than substance.

He was a quiet man. I figured Farmer had been coming in and ordering coffee since the late thirties or early forties. Every morning he'd walk in and the waitress would say, "Coffee?" and he'd just wink yes. (Nodding would have been too vocal for Farmer.) This ritual had been going on for as long as anyone could remember.

It never occurred to me to try to talk to him any more than I would have spoken to the Frederic Remington statue that I passed on the way to school. Maybe I was afraid or maybe it just wasn't meant to be, but I never heard the sound of his voice.

A pretty good myth surrounded Farmer Brown throughout my childhood. If you peeked through the slats in the old barn where he had his saddle shop just at the right angle you could see the back half of a Cadillac hearse sitting there as pretty as you please right next to the bench where Farmer worked. It's also worth mentioning that this hearse was not a junker but a brand-spanking-new 1939 Cadillac hearse. Supposedly it had been sitting right there for the better part of twenty years. You couldn't see all of it, but you could see enough to know somebody had taken such good care of it that it looked like it had just rolled off the showroom floor.

The story behind the hearse seemed to change a little bit with each telling, but the gist of it was basically that Farmer had bought the hearse from the funeral home after it was used to transport his beloved wife to her place of eternal rest. The fascinating part of the story is the fact that Farmer had personally dispatched her and an amorous friend to the hereafter. Apparently it was and may still be legal to do that in Texas (I think since Bush was governor the law now stipulates you have to say "Sorry, hun" before you pull the trigger). However, the resulting guilt was something a man of Farmer's ilk just could not avoid. Talk about your crown of thorns, that big black baby sat right next to him while he worked every day, reminding him for the rest of his life of his (and his dear wife's) unfortunate choices. If I had ever had the nerve to talk to him, I would have asked him if he would have been better served by just killing her lover and scaring the bejesus out of her but allowing her to remain alive. When I think about it, though, I realize that if Farmer had not killed her too, it probably wouldn't have qualified as a legal shooting. It would have been more of a crime of convenience and less of a crime of passion to do it that way. Texas laws are funny like that.

To the boys in our bike posse (think Opie Taylor with cigarettes and small-bore firearms) that hearse was the Holy Grail of used cars, and we all had nightly fantasies about somehow buying it and making the world's greatest hot rod–show car out of it. We talked endlessly of the rarity of that black beauty and all pictured ourselves on the cover of *Hot Rod* magazine sitting at the wheel. Alas, somewhere in the next couple of years the hormonal Mack truck of puberty crushed the fragile dream into a million pieces and only now does a thought of that time resurface.

After all these years I can't help but wonder where that hearse is. Did it take Farmer to his grave when he passed on? I would like to believe it did, but I don't think life is that neat. I also wonder what happened when Farmer got to heaven (I know he went there because he was such a just killer). Were his wife and her lover waiting for him together, or had they been separated when they arrived? Did his wife appreciate his having kept the hearse, or did she think it was stupid? (You just never know what women will think.) Did he have to take the hearse with him for all eternity? (No one has seen it for a long time.) Did the preacher at the Methodist church tell Farmer he thought the hearse-at-work would be a good idea, or did Farmer come up with it himself? Did it really make Farmer feel better, or did it just make him more miserable? Or did he do it to ensure there would never be another woman in his life? If that was the reason, it sure worked. Did the in-laws seek retribution, or did they think she deserved it too? (You just never know.) There are so many unanswered questions.

One thing, however, is for damn sure. If all us aging bike posse guys got together, that hearse would be the main topic of conversation. And I have always believed, no matter how far-fetched it might seem, that people's imaginations develop in an inverse proportion to the amount of color stimulus found in the place they are raised. Our little town produced an inordinate number of really imaginative people who went on to do stuff like invent Styrofoam, dance on the Carol Burnett show, and, yes, even write a pretty good song or two. But it was Farmer Brown who painted the masterpiece in my hometown.

Don Cook

San Antonio–born Don Cook never wanted to be anything but a songwriter. He kicked off his career at the age of fourteen playing with his acoustic folk group in Houston coffeehouses, and he showed up in Nashville three days after graduating from the University of Texas. His early writing incuded such songs as "Tonight," a top-five hit for Barbara Mandrell, and "Lucky Lay Down," which was recorded by John Conlee and became Don's first number-one hit. In 1990, Cook cut some demos for Kix Brooks, with whom he was cowriting, in his home studio. The demos led to Brooks teaming up with Ronnie Dunn for Brooks & Dunn's debut album, Brand New Man, which sold six million copies. Don had eight songs on the album, including the title cut.

Cook has since coproduced thirteen number-one singles for Brooks & Dunn and successful albums with the Mavericks, Alabama, Olivia Newton-John, Shenandoah, Lonestar, Tracy Lawrence, Joe Diffie, David Ball, Rick Trevino, Conway Twitty, and others. His songwriting hits include "It's Getting Better All the Time," "Only in America," "That Ain't No Way to Go," and "You're Gonna Miss Me When I'm Gone," by Brooks & Dunn; "You" by Mark Collie; "What I Meant to Say" and "On a Good Night" by Wade Hayes; "Now I Know" by Lari White; and "Small Town Girl" by Steve Wariner; in addition to cuts by Conway Twitty, George Strait, Keith Whitley, Vince Gill, Alabama, Waylon Jennings, and many others.

In 1994, he was named senior vice-president at Sony/ATV Tree, and four years later received the title of chief creative officer, unprecedented honors for any active songwriter anywhere. In 2004, he retired from the business side of publishing to focus on his family and songwriting.

He Always Knew
Who He Was

Hazel Smith

We're at the airport, fixing to leave for the White House, when Bill shouts, "Hold on, I forgot my briefcase on the bus." Bill's manager, accustomed to undoing Bill's messes, quickly assesses the damage and tells the frazzled woman at the United counter: "Here's the situation: You have before you the Father of Bluegrass Music, Bill Monroe. He's on his way to receive an award from the President. He left his tickets on the tour bus, so you can either hold the plane for about fifteen minutes while I go and get them or let him and his companion board without them." To my surprise, she says: "We'll hold." The manager runs to retrieve Bill's briefcase with our missing tickets and returns shirt untucked, bathed in sweat, and out of breath. He hands the tickets to the woman at the counter, a cart whisks Bill and me to our plane, and we are sipping cocktails in first class fifteen minutes later.

We land in D.C. A limo driver greets us at the gate with a MR. MONROE sign, grabs our carry-ons, and delivers us directly to the front door of the White House. The limo driver opens our door, walks us up the steps, and cordially hands us over to the majordomo standing in the foyer.

"Greetings, Mr. Monroe. The President and Mrs. Clinton as well as the entire staff are honored to have you. Let me briefly fill you in on our presentation schedule," the smiling major-domo says.

"You are the second honoree to arrive. Once all are present, President and Mrs. Clinton will join you for cocktails; they will then escort you to the estate dining room, where you and other dignitaries will dine. After dinner, the President and Mrs. Clinton will escort you to the East Room for your performance. Before I lead you to the Blue Room, where you will meet the other recipients, may I take your coat?"

Bill just stands there.

The majordomo asks again, "Mr. Monroe, may I take your coat?"

"Sure, you got a claim check?"

"But Mr. Monroe, this is the White House."

"I always get a claim check no matter where I am."

"Mr. Monroe, we've never lost anyone's personal effects."

"All the more reason—you're due. I'm not going to be the first one."

For the first time in my life I feel like I could kill Bill for being Bill. The majordomo turns on his heels and marches to a desk near the back wall, opens a drawer, retrieves a piece of White House stationery, creases an inch off the top of the sheet, tears off a three-by-one-inch rectangle, and writes:

THE WHITE HOUSE

CLAIM CHECK

0001

He abruptly turns around, marches back to us, extends the rectangle to Bill, and says, "Mr. Monroe, your claim check. May I take your coat?"

"Where's the stub?"

For the second time in my life I feel like I could kill Bill for being Bill.

"But Mr. Monroe, this is our only claim check."

"Every claim check I've ever seen came with a stub, son. It's no good without it."

At this, the majordomo, sighing audibly, returns to his desk, folds and tears a one-by-one-inch square from a fresh sheet of white house stationery, and writes:

THE WHITE HOUSE

CLAIM CHECK STUB

0001

He walks back looking a little less friendly and hands Bill the stub. Thank you sweet Jesus, Bill finally relinquishes his hat, coat, and briefcase, but looks like he'll bite the MD's arm off when he reaches for his mandolin. The MD is not about to get into another tussle over that. With another audible sigh, the MD passes us off to an aide who escorts Bill, mandolin tucked under his arm, and me to the Blue Room.

The room's empty except for a shortish, fattish elderly man

in a tuxedo and what very well could be a toupee. The elderly man turns around to reveal the aging face of Frank Sinatra. With a grace he's not known for, he glides over, hand extended and all smiles, saying, "Mr. Monroe, I'm Frank Sinatra. When they told me you were going to be one of my fellow honorees, I told Barbara that now I am doubly honored. I may not be able to say I am your biggest fan, but I can honestly say there is not a Bill Monroe album I do not own. You are the only man alive that created a whole music genre."

"What'd you say your name was?" Bill asks.

Crestfallen, Frank sheepishly answers, "Sinatra."

"What do you do?"

"I'm a singer."

"What did you say your name was?"

"Sinatra...Sinatra."

"You know, I think I heard of you."

For the third time in my life, I feel like I *should* kill Bill for being Bill.

Luckily, other honorees and guests begin to swarm into the room and we get a brief reprieve from the icing chill wafting off Frank. Sure enough, the President and Mrs. Clinton eventually show up, just as the majordomo outlined. They work the room, shaking hands with each of us, and then lead us all down to the dining room for a big, fancy supper. The food is good, but we spend most of our time trying to figure out which utensil in a long line of spoons, knives, and forks we are supposed to use. Seems like a dishwashing nightmare to me. Bill pretty much just stabs everything with the biggest knife he can find and mutters to himself a bit. After the last plate is whisked away to our right by the army of white-coated servers, the Clintons lead us to the East Room for the performances.

The first honoree to perform is some world-famous violinist

I've never heard of. I don't catch his name, but I think they say he's from Israel. He stands up on a little six-foot riser and just plays the heart out of his fiddle.

When he finishes, Bill figures Sinatra, the lesser known, will be next, and Bill will close the show. Maybe it's because the drinks are on the house, but Frank has been pounding down scotch since before we arrived and by now he's in no shape to sing, so Bill never gets a chance actually to hear what he sounds like. That makes Bill the second honoree to play. He whips out his mandolin, hunches over, and flails away on the standards he wrote like "Blue Moon of Kentucky" and "Walk Softly on My Heart." He howls in that ghostly, tattered tenor of his and beats the tar out of his battered Gibson F like a man forty years younger. In the middle of "Uncle Pen," Bill shouts out to the Israeli violinist, "Fiddler, do a break."

The fiddler looks around and behind him to see whom Bill's shouting at. Bill nods at him, so there's no doubt whom he's addressing. The fiddler looks horrified and clutches his old fiddle close to his chest. Bill shouts all the louder, "Fiddler, do a break, *do a break*." The fiddler shakes his head and scoots back as far as he can in his seat. Bill shakes his head in disgust as if to say "If I want something done right, I got to do it myself" and beats that poor Gibson all the harder.

After Bill's show, the Clintons say good night and we are all escorted to separate black Lincoln Town Cars. I can tell Bill is a little hot under the collar.

"Sorry I got you into this mess."

"What are your talking about, Bill?"

"I'm talking about this was suppose to be some kind of big deal."

"Bill, this is a big deal. This is as big as it gets. The White House, the Kennedy Award, the President and his wife. What are you talking about?"

"I tell you what I'm talking about. How can it be such a big deal? The singer can't sing and the fiddler can't do a break. I gotta dang near beg to get a proper claim check for my property."

I tell him he's just feeling ornery and he cools down for a bit and we get a good night's sleep.

The next day, everything goes as planned. They pick us up early and shuttle us from the luncheon to a banquet and then another big gala award ceremony. The fiddler, steering clear of us, does the same song he played last night. Bill plows through a half dozen of his hits in a flurry of pickin' and singing. He's just getting warmed up when the President joins him onstage to address the crowd. Bill receives his award first because he's already up there. The fiddler and Sinatra are next, and it's obvious to me that they are trying not to stand too close to Monroe; it's equally obvious that this arrangement is just fine with Bill.

We're at the airport bright and early the next morning when Bill's briefcase goes through the security X-ray machine. You'd think that it was the day of rapture or hell had indeed broken loose. Alarms blaring, security people running, Bill pinned against the wall by a policeman while three others start fussing with his case. Inside the briefcase, swaddled in a Crown Royal bag, is a Colt revolver.

"Mr. Monroe, where did you get this gun?"

"A fan gave it to me."

"Somebody in the airport asked you to carry this gun?"

"No, you fool—a fan at a show in Little Rock thirty years ago."

"Why are you carrying this gun with you?"

"I won't take two steps without it. I always carry my gun. In my business, a man never knows when he's going to need a persuader like this."

"Mr. Monroe, did you realize this gun is loaded?"

"Well, it ain't worth a dang if it ain't."

"Mr. Monroe, can you tell us where you have been while in Washington?"

"The White House."

"The White House? As in the residency of the President of the United States?"

"Well, what other White House do you think I'd be talking about?"

"Mr. Monroe, do have any proof that you have been to the White House?"

At which point Bill reaches into his pocket and pulls out a crumpled rectangle, on which is written:

**THE WHITE HOUSE
CLAIM CHECK STUB
0001**

There is a pause while all the security personnel gather around the torn scrap of paper and talk in hushed tones. Finally, the one asking all the questions says, "I'm sorry, Mr. Monroe, you are going to have to miss your flight. We have some more questions to ask you."

"Whoa, son, wait a minute. I'm Bill Monroe. I'm the Father of Bluegrass Music and I've got to play the Opry tonight. I'm getting on that plane."

Well, I guess that's the thing about Bill. He may not know who Frank Sinatra is but he always knows who Bill Monroe is.

Hazel Smith

Hazel Smith moved from Caswell County, North Carolina, with her sons and her "stuff" in a pickup truck to Nashville in 1970. After about a year of doing "anything she could find to feed them," she found work in the music business, eventually in the employ of Tompall Glaser, whose partner was Waylon Jennings.

In 1973 Smith coined the phrase "outlaw music" to define the self-produced, hard-driving music Jennings, Willie Nelson, Kris Kristofferson, and all the hat-bearing cowboys were recording. The name stuck, and in 1976, Wanted! The Outlaws, *a compilation record by Jennings, his wife, Jessi Colter, Nelson, and Glaser, became the first certified platinum record by country artists. A songwriter in her own right, Smith was also the subject of Bill Monroe's "Walk Softly on My Heart."*

For thirty years, she wrote a column for Country Music *magazine until its demise, when she began writing for* Country Weekly *and, more recently, for the weekly "Hot Dish" column on CMT.com. She's authored a cookbook,* Hazel's Hot Dish: Cookin' with Country Stars, *and has appeared on Emeril Lagasse's* Emeril Live, *and on more episodes of* The Ellen DeGeneres Show *than any other guest. Smith has been heard daily on WFMS Radio in Indianapolis for fourteen years, and twice weekly on KUSS in San Diego. She currently hosts the CMT television show* Southern Fried Flicks with Hazel Smith.

In 1999 Smith received the highest award in country music journalism when the Country Music Association (CMA) named her recipient of the Media Achievement Award. Smith calls this her proudest moment.

Curtis Loach

Charlie Daniels

I'm a man who has done a pretty good bit of traveling in his day. I been to New York City, and I been to Miami, Florida. I been to Charlotte and Richmond and Greensboro. I mean, I ain't just some feller you'd see on the street and say to yourself, "I bet that feller has traveled a lot." I ain't wearing no travel stickers on my forehead or nothing, but I was even in New Orleans, Louisiana, one time.

I also ain't trying to say that I know everything in the world they is to know, but I have been out of New Hanover County a couple of times. I guess what I'm trying to say is, of all the people I've seen (Oh! I went to Atlanta to a baseball game, too, a major league baseball game), in all them places I've been, I'd have to say that the downright damnedest man I ever did see was Curtis Loach.

He used to do and say the beatingest things of anybody in the world.

I mean, you take the time that his youngest son was born. Curtis claimed to be part Cherokee Indian. (I never did believe he was.) Anyway, Curtis said that he was gonna do like the

Indians used to do and name his baby for the first thing he seen after the child was born.

Well, the first thing he seen was a can of paint, so he named the poor little boy Hi-Glo, Hi-Glo Loach. How would you like to drag that name around with you for the rest of your life?

And he was always telling jokes that he made up hisself. And they never were a damn bit funny.

He'd say something like, "Knock, knock."

"Who's there?"

"Alley."

"Alley who?"

"Alley Bamy," and then he'd bust out laughing like he was Bob Hope or something.

And if you was standing in front of him when he laughed, he'd spit all over you. He kinda gurgled and sounded like a commode flushing, with just about as much water. It was a downright disgusting habit.

I remember one time at a high school football game when the referee called back a touchdown that our boys made, and our whole side of the field was up hollering. I mean, everybody in town was madder than hell. Well, that won't good enough for Mr. Curtis Loach. He was drunk as a fiddler's bitch, and he went running out on the field and called the referee a blind pissant. Then he picked up the football and let the air out of it with his pocketknife.

And I think one of the worst things that he done was he called everybody "Sweets": "How you doing, Sweets?" "Well, all right, Sweets." "I'll see you later, Sweets." It was aggravating as hell just to be around him.

Curtis never did own a car, but he had an old wore-out Ford tractor, and he'd drive that thing all over the place. He'd even drive it to town on Saturday.

Curtis lived in a mighty run-down old place about three miles out of town. It leaned to one side and he never did cut the grass in the yard. It used to get knee-deep in the summertime.

His wife used to have a baby every year. They must have had ten or eleven children. Their yard was always full of snotty-nosed kids running around and hollering and carrying on. If you drove up in the yard, they'd all jump right in your car and act like they was driving and go all through your glove compartment.

One time, Glen Gooden left the keys in his pickup truck, and one of them little kids got it started up and run it right into the side of the house. Knocked part of the front porch down, and that's the way it stayed. And Glen had to spend a pocketful of his own money to get his truck fixed. Hell, he knew that there won't no use in trying to make Curtis and that hungry brood of his pay for it.

I remember that Curtis's old milk cow used to get out all the time and get into Mrs. Mildred Bennett's garden. Mr. Bennett told Curtis that the next time his cow got into Mrs. Mildred's garden, he was gonna pull all her upper teeth. Well, sure enough, the old cow got out again, and when Curtis went to pick her up, he looked in her mouth. Naturally, the cow didn't have no upper teeth. Curtis got mad as hell and was threatening to shoot Mr. Bennett, till somebody told him what any fool knows: cows don't have no upper teeth anyway.

He was a mess, but I'd have to say that Curtis Loach was also about the happiest feller I did ever did see.

Well, one day a man showed up in town. He was real dressed up and talked with a Yankee accent and was asking around about how to get to Curtis Loach's place. Nobody knew who he was or what he wanted, but we gave him the directions. It turned out that he was a big lawyer from Chicago, Illinois.

It seemed that Curtis's granddaddy had come from Oklahoma and had owned an old no-account piece of farmland out there, and damned if they hadn't found oil on the place. Curtis, being the next of kin, owned the place now. Just like that, Curtis Loach was as rich as all get out. I'm talking about filthy rich.

Now, here was an ignorant dirt farmer that never did have two nickels to rub together, and all of a sudden, overnight, he came into millions of dollars. I mean, the man gave him a check for $250,000 just for signing the papers.

Well, all hell busted aloose in our little part of the world.

The next morning Curtis went to town and bought him one of them big diesel tractors, and nobody was safe on the roads after that. He was roaring around town on that damn monstrosity, just generally terrorizing everybody, running up on the sidewalk and all. He run right into the light pole in front of the hardware store and knocked off half the electric power in town. He broke the light pole clean in two and didn't even slow down, just kept right on going.

When Sheriff Cox finally caught up with him and told him he was gonna have to pay for that light pole, Curtis pulled out a wad of cash money big enough to choke a mule and peeled off a big handful of hundred-dollar bills. He handed them over and said, "Ed, if that ain't enough, you know where to find me!"

Then he started buying things. He bought eight color televisions, three refrigerators, a washer and dryer, two living room suites (one for him and one for his wife), a haybaler, a thrashing machine, a corn picker, all kinds of discs and turn plows, fourteen shotguns, an electric stove with a self-cleaning oven, and he bought Simmon's grocery store slam out of Popsicles. Damn if he didn't even buy a used bulldozer. He just went crazy.

Curtis Loach would buy just about anything that anybody would sell him. You couldn't even get close to his house for the salesmen. They were all over the place, coming from as far away as Virginia, selling everything from Cadillacs to sewing machines. Curtis and his family went through money like it was falling from the sky, but them oil wells in Oklahoma went on pumping and the money just kept on rolling in.

One day he decided he didn't like the music on the radio, so he bought the radio station to "put some decent music on the air." From sunup till sundown, all you could hear was Curtis's favorite songs. He liked bluegrass, and it was Bill Monroe and Flatt and Scruggs all day long.

His yard was full of swing sets, his fields were full of farm machinery, his pastures were full of prize cows, and his house was full of every kind of gadget you could imagine. He couldn't have squeezed another thing into that dilapidated old place with a shoehorn.

It was dangerous to even be around Curtis's neighborhood. His wife wrecked three brand-new Lincoln Continentals trying to learn how to drive. And she never did learn how. She finally just give up, and the three wrecked cars set out on the shoulder of the road in front of his house.

Even with all the aggravation of Curtis driving all over the place in a super-charged diesel tractor, endangering life, limb, and property, and in spite of all the mess that Curtis Loach's newfound wealth brought into our lives, I'll have to say that we done a damn good job of enduring it all. That is, we did until some fool sold Curtis Loach an airplane.

It was a single-engine job, and Curtis took about three hours' worth of flying lessons, and then the skies over our part of the world became unsafe for birds. Imagine living in a town where a man who couldn't even drive a car would come flying an airplane over your house at 150 feet at twelve o'clock at night. It was nerve-wracking as hell.

I'll have to say one thing for Curtis, though. He looked after his family. He bought his wife a full-length white mink coat. It would have looked real good, but she dipped snuff and was always spitting down the front of it. After a while, it looked like hell.

What all of us couldn't figure out was why somebody would buy one of everything in the world and live in a house where the rain fell right through the roof. But we didn't have to wonder long.

Curtis hauled off and built him a house like you wouldn't believe. It must have had thirty rooms. Everything was electrified. It had a swimming pool and tennis court (Curtis didn't know a damn thing about tennis). It had three acres of the prettiest, greenest lawn you ever have seen. It was built out of fine stone with a paved circular drive.

It had a reading room, sitting room, drawing room, den, dining room, blue room, living room, full basement, gymnasium, sauna, hot tub, solarium, library, gun room, and a monstrous-sized kitchen. It was three stories of unadulterated fanciness, with six half-baths and eight full baths, with enclosed shower stalls and king-size sunken bathtubs. Now, for a family whose facility had been some thirty yards from the back door and the biggest luxury there was the Sears and Roebuck catalog, that was a pretty fancy place to answer a call of nature.

The grounds had a greenhouse, a putting green, an archery range, guest house, eight-car garage, servants' quarters, and I forgot to mention the whirlpool alongside of the regular heated, chlorinated, Olympic-size swimming pool.

The paneling in the drawing room used to be in some Catholic church in Italy or somewhere, and a lot of the furniture was named after Looey something or other—some dead French king.

There was a dumbwaiter in the kitchen that served all the

floors and an intercom system that would play music all over the house.

There was a chandelier in the living room that was bigger than a two-horse wagon wheel, with little diamondlike things just dripping off of it.

There was a burglar alarm, fire alarm, floodlights, riding stable, and the gun room had a fireplace that was eight foot across and four and a half foot high, made out of native stone.

It was the fanciest, most uppity-looking, awesome, efficient, centrally heated and air-conditioned structure since the Taj Mahal.

Curtis had an announcement made over his radio station for everybody to come by and see it the day they moved in. Needless to say, all the women in the town would have done anything short of killing to get a look inside Curtis's palace, and the men weren't a whole lot different, so damn near the whole town showed up that day.

It was like going to Disneyland. I mean, he had his own regulation-sized pool table and one of them televisions with the great big screen on it. It was a sight to see. That house was all, and I mean *all,* that anybody ever talked about.

"Did you notice that Weatherby .300 magnum in the gun cabinet?" Or "Gladys, she had a walk-in cooler right in the kitchen with sides of beef hanging in it." I mean, that's all you heard.

We didn't see much of Curtis in those days. Somebody said he was trying to learn how to play golf. After about six months, he showed up down at the pool room one night, right before closing time. He didn't try to tell no jokes and didn't even get on nobody's nerves. It was just, "Howdy, fellers," and he just sat at the bar and drank his beer.

Norman, I believe it was, said after a while, "How you liking the house, Curtis?"

"It's all right," Curtis mumbled.

"Did you watch the Cowboys game on that big TV?"

"Naw."

"Somebody told me you had a horse up there that cost $100,000 dollars."

"Damn ole thoroughbred. Can't ride the son of a bitch."

"Curtis, Graham Fowler told me that you had ten full-time hands working up there."

"I can't understand a word that butler feller says, and if I get up to go to the bathroom at night, when I come back, the damn sheets has been changed. And that woman that cooks can mess up a pot of beans worse than anybody I ever seen."

I think that it dawned on everybody at about the same time—I know it did on me—that Curtis Loach was about the most miserable feller I ever did see. He took to spending his days going down to the old house and sitting on the porch. I seen him at the drugstore one day and it seemed like he walked a little slower and his hair was a little grayer.

We was playing Clarkton one Friday night, and I mean it was an intense game. We scored right before the half, but the jackass in a zebra suit called interference on our boys and brought it back, so we went into halftime tied nothing to nothing.

Somebody said, "Remember that night that old Curtis Loach run out on the field and busted the football? Life ain't been the same around here since Curtis got rich." We all agreed that maybe some of his jokes might even have been a little bit funny.

Did you ever have one of them déjà vu things happen to you? I mean where you feel like you know everything that's gonna happen right down to the words people are gonna say? Well, one of them clicked in on me right about then. I heard it in my head before I heard it in my ears. A kind of a *waughhhhhh* sound from a way off, and it kept getting louder and closer.

All of a sudden from out of the night and into the lights of the football field there came a big green diesel tractor. There's a cyclone fence at the north end zone, and he just plowed right on through it.

There was cheerleaders and band players running, and Curtis Loach, as drunk as a fiddler's bitch, came driving onto the football field. He drove right out to the fifty-yard line and stopped. Damn if the crowd didn't give him a standing ovation, and then he rode around the field one time and drove away.

Boy! That crowd was so up and cheered so hard for our boys that we beat Clarkton thirty-one to nothing. It was a fine old night.

The next day it was in the Raleigh paper that the government was filing a multimillion-dollar tax-fraud suit against Curtis Loach. It seems that Curtis had never filed an income tax return in his whole life. He just didn't know that you were supposed to. He started attracting attention when he started making all that money, but the IRS had never heard of him.

They audited and audited and figured and figured, and when they got done it turned out that all Curtis was gonna get to keep was his old farm, his new house, and that diesel tractor he thought so much of.

They told him, "Mr. Loach, it looks like were gonna have to take just about everything you've got."

They said old Curtis jumped up and laughed and said, "Come get it."

That big house they lived in has changed a considerable amount. The grass in the yard is about knee high. Almost all of the glass has been broke out of the greenhouse, and Curtis keeps a litter of bluetick hound puppies in the drawing room. The swimming pool is green and that bunch of little monsters have tore the dumbwaiter all to hell riding up and down in it. And the yard is full of snotty-nosed kids all running around and hollering and carrying on.

And I believe that Curtis Loach is the happiest feller I ever did see.

Charlie Daniels

Born in 1936 in Wilmington, North Carolina, Charlie Daniels was raised on a musical diet that included Pentecostal gospel, local bluegrass bands, rhythm and blues, and country music.

His résumé includes recording sessions with artists as diverse as Bob Dylan, Flatt and Scruggs, Pete Seeger, Mark O'Connor, Leonard Cohen, Ringo Starr, and Johnny Cash. His 1979 Grammy Award–winning song, "The Devil Went Down to Georgia," has earned numerous accolades, including three Country Music Association trophies. He earned a Dove Award from the Gospel Music Association in 1994 for The Door, *and a 1997 CMA nomination for his remake of "Long Haired Country Boy" featuring John Berry and Hal Ketchum.*

As an author, Daniels published a collection of short stories, The Devil Went Down to Georgia, *peopled with the same kind of characters and tall tales as his songs.*

"I used to say, 'I'm not an outlaw; I'm an outcast,'" says the multi-platinum star. "When it gets right down to the

nitty-gritty, I've just tried to be who I am. I've never followed trends or fads. I couldn't even if I tried. I can't be them; I can't be anybody but me."

Daniels's world-famous annual Volunteer Jam concerts have always featured a variety of current stars and heritage artists and are considered by historians his most impressive contribution to Southern music. In April 1998, top stars and two former presidents paid tribute to Daniels when he was named the recipient of the Pioneer Award at the Academy of Country Music's annual nationally televised ceremonies. You can visit his Web site at www.charliedaniels.com.

The Elk Hunters

Tim Johnson

We drove three hours in my dad's '74 Ford four-wheel drive, drinking black coffee from thermoses and eating maple bars we bought at the Noti grocery store the day before. Dad was at the wheel, as always. Napping on the way to our hunting spot was almost impossible, with my brother, Mark, and my father chain-smoking: one Winstons, the other Pall Malls. Mark took pity on me and let me have the window seat so that I could sit nearer to some breathable air. All it really did was draw the smoke over to my side and make my right shoulder cold. It was, after all, 5:00 A.M. on an early September day and still over an hour until sunrise. This was the time we caught up on each other's life and relived the glory days of high school wrestling, female conquests, and hunts from years gone by. Dad mostly listened to our stories (he knew them all), and he would occasionally interject "Bullshit" or chuckle whenever we exaggerated the details. I recall he laughed a lot on those drives.

We were an odd-looking trio bound together as much by blood as by twenty-five years of hunting trips just like this one. On this trip, we were dressed in a haphazard ensemble of camouflage and flannel. Dad was wearing his black felt hat with the rattlesnake skin he had worn since I can remember. Mark had on a camo hat, and I wore a dark blue ball cap with the letters BMI. We looked nothing like the pro hunters on the sportsman channel, but we were fine with that. In our provincial minds, we were serious elk hunters.

The three of us traded rifle hunting for bow hunting back in '85, after my dad quarreled with another elk hunter—an altercation that nearly ended in tragedy for the other guy. Apparently, Dad had made a clean kill on a four-point bull and was just about to field-dress it when another hunter approached and insisted he had shot the elk. After a rather lengthy and heated argument, Dad let the other hunter claim the kill. It's a little like winning the lottery and having some jerk snatch the ticket out of your hand. The average elk hunter gets one elk about every seven years. One mature bull elk weighs about 1,100 pounds and can give you as much as 300 pounds of meat, enough to feed your family for a year or more. Needless to say, Dad was steamed. When he got to the landing of the freshly logged unit, he could see the elk thief struggling with the carcass on the hillside, obviously "some stupid sonovabitch from Eugene with a dull knife" and clearly not up to the task at hand. Dad said he had him in his crosshairs for over ten minutes and was contemplating putting a 30-06 hollow point through his brain until he thought better of it and drove off.

Whenever Dad told this story, I could see him reliving his anger. His lips would flatten out and he would squint like Clint Eastwood did in *Dirty Harry* when confronting a low-life desperado. Then his face would relax and he would say that the outside chance of getting caught and spending his life in the pen had changed his mind. I always thought it was funny that the threat of prison time kept him from pulling the trigger and not that the actual killing would have been wrong. Mark once remarked after hearing this tale, "I would have blown his fucking head off." But I know he wouldn't have. He was a tough logger and a great fighter, but he was no murderer. If I had walked in my dad's shoes that day, I can't be certain what my reaction would have been. The injustice of losing a big bull elk would have been hard for me to handle. The biggest elk I had ever bagged was a spike. A few days later my dad was on that very same landing and saw the buzzards feasting on what he thought were the entrails from the bull, but when he spied the kill through his binoculars, he could plainly see that the hunter had left the meat to rot on the ground and taken the head for a trophy. I can understand that in the heat of the moment, many men (perhaps even I) would fantasize about pulling the trigger.

My father and brother were still residents of Oregon, and in fact always would be. They were cut from the same cloth. Both had been loggers and both of them had little to show for years of risking their lives in the forests of the coastal mountain range in western Oregon. Loggers live in the present, and spend their money like there's not a future. For a lot of them, there isn't.

I had been living in Nashville, Tennessee, for about ten years, making a fairly good living as a songwriter. I had my first hit in '95, a song called "Whys, Lies and Alibis," and since then had had a couple of number-one-charting songs and a few that made it onto the top-ten list. I owe much of my earlier music education to my father and his eight-track cassette player. He had a selection of about ten artists: Charley Pride, Merle Haggard, Willie Nelson, Waylon Jennings, Kris Kristofferson, and Ray Charles were among my favorites. After listening to Bobby Goldsboro warble "Little Green Apples" a thousand times, even his over-the-top vibrato didn't bother me. Dad was such a racist that it always surprised me that he kept Ray Charles in his glove box. I could understand his affection for Charlie Pride's music, primarily because he didn't sound "black" and I think there were a lot of people that didn't know that he was, but Ray was the epitome of a black singer. Maybe the music was so great even my redneck father had to ignore his skin color. Rural Oregon doesn't have a large African-American population (less than one percent), so I can't be sure my father ever met a black person. No matter, he hated them all.

My success in the music business was a source of great pride for my family, especially my brother. I was not rich, but I made enough to be able to afford the annual out-of-state tag and license fee, which added up to about $750—money well spent, especially if we got an elk. We always shared whatever elk we got as a group, so we rooted for anyone to fill their tag. Elk tastes like a blend of deer meat and beef. It's much more flavorful than beef and a lot less gamey than deer. It is a highly coveted commodity among those who live in the foothills of the Willamette Valley. Most hunters in Oregon butcher and package their own game, unlike those in Tennessee, where the hunters take their deer, skin and all, to a processing plant. This is the reason most of the venison I have eaten in Tennessee tastes gamey. The processors don't take the time to remove the thin tough membrane from the muscles that some folks call silver skin. My father calls it striffing, but regardless of the name, it's the stuff that gives it that strong, wild, and unpleasant flavor. Butchering an elk is tedious work, but it pays off in the end because you are left with delicious and completely organic meat that you can use in any dish that calls for beef.

We pulled a little beat-up camper that I affectionately called our fleabag motel on wheels. It could sleep two comfortably and had a little kitchenette with a small refrigerator that allowed us to enjoy hot meals (chili, stew, venison) and perk our coffee for the day's hunt. Mark and I would take turns sleeping in the front seat of the truck, where it was a constant battle to get comfortable because of the steering wheel and the gear shift. It didn't matter which end my head was at—the seat was just too small for a man almost six feet tall. My neck and back would be so stiff in the morning that it took thirty minutes and three cups of Mark's strong java before I could stand up straight. Mark, who is five inches shorter and thirty pounds lighter, would often take mercy on me and take two of three nights in the truck, but I always had to endure his insults ("lightweight," "girlie-man," etc.). He didn't want me to think that he was a nice guy or a pushover. I guess it was part of the unspoken macho logger code I wasn't privy to. He would have let me spend the whole time in the camper, but I didn't want to appear too soft, even though we all knew I was.

We pulled over and unhitched the camper at a park site in the Siuslaw National Forest, which was our usual base camp, and continued on high into the mountains, with which my brother and dad were so familiar. I would ask where we were going, and my brother would say, "Where the big ones are," then nod his head, cluck his tongue, and take another drag off his Winston. Dad would then give me the road and the unit number: "Up on B-19, near Hate Creek." I preferred my brother's answer, vague but always imaginative. Dad's answer, although accurate, made me feel a little like an outsider, an interloper in a world in which I did not belong. The truth hurt.

The first day of the hunt is always full of excitement and wonder. Will we see a big herd with bulls and sneak up on them? Will one cross in front of us on the road and make us pile out of the truck and run into the brush? Will we see fresh scat or tracks and start stalking them? Will I get the chance to pull back on my bow and let an arrow fly? Rarely do we bag an elk (if we get one at all) on the first day, and for me the annual trip became less about killing an elk and more about spending quality time with my brother and father. Eventually, this would be my only chance to see them. The better my career was going and the more money I was making, the more it seemed to squeeze my available time into smaller increments. For me, this was ten short days of vacation; for my dad and Mark this was the beginning of a month-long season. My dad and Mark had the luxury of patience. I wanted to have some action, so I could tell my wife, Laura, wild stories of our adventures. Also, I suppose I needed to justify leaving her behind in Nashville, and to somehow alleviate my guilt of going on an expensive and selfish man-trip. Laura seemed to understand my need to reconnect with my family. She was always supportive, but she would often remind me of these solo trips during arguments. This sustained my insecurity about taking such trips but not to the extent that I didn't take them. The truth is, I wouldn't miss them for anything.

As we made our way up the narrow logging roads, I could make out the headlights of other trucks across the canyons and along the ridges. Knowing we weren't the only bow hunters in the area made my pulse race, but my two companions didn't seem to be worried at all. I wondered out loud if we should have left earlier, and Mark looked at Dad and shook his head like that might have been the stupidest question ever posed in the history of all human existence. "Fuck, bro, we're going to the Hole," he barked. "Only I know where that is. Quit your sniveling."

"I'm not sniveling, just wondering," I sniveled. Everybody laughed, especially Dad.

Ten minutes later, Mark told Dad to turn left down an old cat road, which he did dutifully. "Here it is, boys, the Hole."

Mark knew these roads better than anyone because he still made his living out here. He logged the Hole a couple of years ago, and saw herds of elk every single day. He was head rigger on one of International Paper's hottest logging crews. Dad had logged these forests thirty years before, and the terrain had changed considerably. We all trusted that Mark would get us to the Hole, where the big elk thrived.

Dad turned off the truck and the heater made what could best be described as a death rattle. The very same rattle it had been making for years. We could see the definition in the Douglas fir in the skyline and we all knew in thirty or so minutes it would be light enough for us to see through our binoculars onto the hillsides and landings. The elk would still be feeding on the mountain grasses, maples, and salal brush in the cool morning air. Once the sun comes up, they will find familiar beds beneath new-growth firs or brushy maples that shade them from the sun. When they have bedded down, spotting them becomes extremely difficult. Hunters then have to rely on other signs, such as fresh tracks, scat, antler rubbings, broken foliage, old trails, and sometimes even an elk's scent, which is a strong musky odor, distinct and not terribly unpleasant, at least not for the elk and their human predators.

We took our bows and knives out of the back of Dad's truck and Mark instructed me which spur road to walk down. He took the cat road that led into the old growth. Dad would drive up the road and scope the freshly logged units. His weak heart did not let him do a lot of walking up steep roads and canyons. It gave him angina, which was painful and probably scary. He always carried nitro pills with him, but he would rather not have to use them. It was another reason he didn't enjoy hunting alone these days, I suspected. We would meet back in a couple of hours, unless someone saw elk, in which case he would signal on his walkie-talkie. Then we would try to coordinate the hunt. Until that point, we were in "finding the elk mode."

The temperature, in the mid-forties at 6 A.M., would climb into the eighties by eleven and make it nearly unbearable for everyone, animals included, so I relished these next three or four hours, and have always considered them the best hunting time. I carried my bow in both hands and had an arrow ready to go in case I needed to get off a quick shot. Normally, I wouldn't load an arrow unless I was certain elk were imminent. Since this was the first day, I was not especially optimistic.

People sometimes have the misconception that the bows we use are the similar to the ones used by Native Americans, but that's not true. Modern bows are not primitive wood/leather/obsidian/eagle feather contraptions. These are precision high-tech compound bows that can shoot a carbon fiberglass arrow with a razor-sharp titanium tip 338 feet per second. If you are close enough (thirty to forty yards) to the elk, the arrow can actually pass entirely through an adult elk's body. I have a very nice Mathews bow, but it's by no means state-of-the-art. My brother, however, must have spent an entire paycheck on his pricey and powerful Mathews Black Max.

I have never been one of those rabid hunters like you see on TV, dressed like a tree and smelling of elk urine, bugling in an eight-point bull aching for a fight during rut (the mating season), jumping out from behind a rock or bush and making the kill shot. Clearly, I'm no Ted Nugent. That is not to say I'm not passionate about the hunt, because I am. I just save my unbridled enthusiasm for writing songs.

I spent two hours that morning walking, stopping, listening, and looking at hillsides and canyons in the Hole. I saw five deer, two hawks, numerous chipmunks and songbirds, and a covey of quail that got my adrenaline flowing. When they flew up into the air all at once, it sounded like a Black Hawk helicopter taking off. I sucked wind and jumped back noisily. I was certain any elk in the area made note of my arrival and ducked into the forest or slipped farther into the cover of those brushy maples. This was the game; I knew the rules before I bought my ticket. In the absence of fresh signs of elk, I sat on a stump, ate an apple, and marveled at the beauty of my surroundings. I swatted at the occasional yellow jacket with little success, and decided to find my father and Mark and plan the rest of our day.

As I walked back the way I came, I saw Dad's familiar truck and those unmistakable spotlights on the cab of the truck above the windshield. They hadn't worked in years, but Dad hadn't bothered to remove them. As I approached, I saw a man in a green uniform leaning into the driver's-side window. It was a game warden.

I panicked and reached into my pocket for my wallet, certain I had left it at home along with my license and tag. But it was in my back pocket and when I looked up, my dad and the warden were watching. I expect the warden sees that kind of reaction all season long.

"Hey," the warden said with a half smile.

"Hey," I replied. I introduced myself and offered my hand. He seemed a little surprised, but shook it firmly.

"Did you see anything?" he asked.

"No, nothing of consequence," I said. There was a four-or-five-second pause as he considered my answer.

"From out of state?" he inquired, eyebrows raised, and I realized that I must have brought some of my Southern accent with me. The funny thing was that I now noticed the Northwest accent of my family in Oregon—the same one I had brought to and mostly lost while living in Nashville. Apparently, I had only replaced my "Fargo" accent (as Laura calls it) with a drawl.

"My boy here is from Tennessee," Dad said through the open window. "He's a songwriter."

I was taken back by my dad's interjection into the conversation, and completely mystified as to why he would offer up my occupation when it was absolutely irrelevant to the situation. My father is a softspoken man who has few words for anyone, especially strangers. Then, to my surprise, he continued on with more information.

"My other boy works in these woods," he added. "He'll be back shortly, I'm guessing." If I hadn't known better, I'd have said Dad was nervous about something.

I gave the warden my tag and license without waiting for him to ask, and he gave it a cursory look and handed it back to me. I realized he'd had no intention of asking me for it, but was trying to be polite or trying to seem professional. We leaned up against the truck and chitchatted about the weather and the forest fires during the summer. Everyone was relieved that we'd had a few weeks of rain prior to the opening day of elk season. They had shut down large areas of the national forest last year, which pushed all the elk hunters into the same region. Bow hunters like their privacy, so for them, the rain was an answered prayer.

"So, what kind of songs do you write?" he asked out of the blue. I had been pretty sure he hadn't heard my father, but I was wrong.

"Country, mostly," I said, hoping to end this part of the conversation. No luck, however.

"I really don't listen to much country," he said, "but I do like that song about that guy's mama getting runned over by a damned old train."

Everyone that hates country music remembers that Steve Goodman song, "You Don't Have to Call Me by My Name," also recorded under the title, "The Perfect Country Song," sung by David Allan Coe. It is what most of those people think every country song is about: lying, cheating, drinking, or dogs. It was hard for me to argue, having penned "Whys, Lies and Alibis" as my first hit. I faked a smile and said, "Yeah, wish I had written it."

The warden was turning to leave when he looked back and said offhand, "Oh, you heard they found that missing hunter?"

"I didn't know one was missing," I said. "Already?"

"No, no." He laughed. "That missing hunter back in the mid-eighties. Another game warden found his skull over on some Umpqua unit last week. Still had a slug of some kind rattling around in it."

I was confused. "A slug?" I asked stupidly.

"Yeah, you know...a bullet," he replied.

"So he was killed?"

"Well, they don't know yet. Might have been an accident. But if it was, someone also accidentally buried him in a shallow grave. There were some other bones around the area, mostly elk. Hard to say how old those were. But you don't have to be a member of CSI to figure out what happened there. Folks can get downright nasty about a downed elk. You fellas have good luck and be safe out here." He waved to my dad and walked up the road to his little Dodge truck with the tree on it.

Maybe if I hadn't caught my father's look in the side mirror, I never would have connected the dots. His face was completely white, every molecule of blood drained from his forehead to his chin. It hit me like that train hit that guy's mama in that song. Guilt. Remorse. Abject fear. Dad's old story played over in my mind. The look he got when he got to the bad parts of the tale. How could my dad have killed another human being over an elk? My God, my father was a murderer. My knees were beginning to take a vacation of their own and I had to grab the rear bumper to hold myself up or I might have collapsed right there in the dirt. The story I had heard for years, and practically had memorized, was nothing but a well-told lie. Or at least the important parts were. The ending was radically different than I ever could have imagined. It was as if instead of Goldilocks running home and never venturing in the woods by herself again, she was really torn limb from limb by those three angry bears and fed to the foxes.

What seemed like hours went by before my father finally opened the door and walked around front to urinate. He began nodding his head up and down as he came back. I knew he was going to confess to the crime. His dirty secret was out, and there would be no denial. Apparently he got a look at my reaction as well. This is why I avoid Texas Hold 'Em. A poker face is not my forté.

"All right, son, I'm not going to bullshit you." A forever pause while he lit a Pall Mall with his Bic lighter and stuck it in his red and green flannel shirt. He took a monster drag off the cigarette and said, "I killed him. I killed that sonovabitch and I never lost one night's sleep over it. I felt bad for his family later, but if there ever was a man that needed killing, it was him." He walked over to where I had slumped against the rear wheel. "I'm gonna tell you what happened and you can make your own judgment, but you promise this stays between you and me. Your brother doesn't need to know any of this." He waited for my response and got none. "Promise!" he yelled.

"What the fuck, Dad, what the fuck." I was reduced to a blithering idiot. I couldn't promise a murderer anything. I wasn't prepared or equipped to deal with this kind of thing. I admit part of me was scared that if I didn't promise to keep my mouth shut, there on the spot, I'd wind up like the missing hunter. I imagined the conversation he'd have with Mark: "Oh I don't know where Tim went, Mark. Maybe we should wait for the buzzards to start circling." I felt myself hyperventilating.

Dad opened the tailgate and took out the cooler. He took out two Miller Lites and used the cooler for his seat. He handed me one of them. "All right, son, calm down. You don't have to promise shit. I don't want you to tell Mark, and I'll just have to hope you have the good sense not to. Here's what happened. What really happened." An even longer drink of alcohol followed a long drag of nicotine.

"I was rifle hunting by myself up on the Umpqua, and it was a nasty rainy-ass day. I wasn't even going to go but your mom and I were fighting and I had to get out of the house. I was on unit 16-F looking at the timberline when I spotted a five-point bull—a beauty. He was only standing about 150 yards away. He turned broadside on me and I let him have it right behind the front shoulders with my 30-06. He went ass over teakettle down the ridge and rolled up against a fir stump. I knew he was dead—I watched him for ten to fifteen minutes and he didn't move a muscle. Well, I knew getting that big SOB out was going to be hard, but I got my cable ready and drug it out as far as I could. I was going to quarter the elk and carry him to the end of the cable and get it out that way. It wasn't gonna be fun, but I had plenty of daylight and I would have been home before supper. I had already field-dressed the bull and was taking a break under a tree when I heard shots—oh I don't know, maybe three or four. Then I heard some guy whooping it up. I took out my binoculars and I spotted him on a lower landing from where I was. I figured he took out another satellite bull, and I was thinking what lucky bastards we were, and how rare it was to get two bulls out of the same canyon on the same day.

That's where I figured wrong. I saw him coming up the ridge towards my bull, and thought he must need my help or something, but the truth is, he never saw me till thirty minutes later when he walked up on my bull and me. I never had a chance to say hey how are you or nothing when he said 'What the hell are you doing?' I told him I was trying to get my elk out when he said, 'Your elk?' Well, he was convinced he'd killed this elk, and even when I showed him the blood on the ground and on the little elms where the elk had rolled down the hill, and the place where I shot the bull on its right side, he either didn't believe me or he just plain didn't want to. I felt sorry for him, at first. I could see things were getting out of control, and even though I didn't want to, I offered to split the elk with him. I even offered to use my tag. He could have hunted the rest of the season with half an elk in his freezer. He had a crazy look on his face, and suddenly I found myself looking down the barrel of his gun. I believe it was a 30-30. I admit I was scared. I guess I wasn't hiding my fear too good, 'cause I saw this smile come over his face. I thought he was gonna kill me right then and there. I dropped to my knees and I started begging for my life."

I sipped my beer and listened to my dad's story intently. I was in shock from the admission of murder, but I think I was more flabbergasted by the sheer amount of detail and sentences strung together by a man known for one-word explanations. He was looking at his cork boots while he was recounting the events of that day. His expression never changed until he continued on with the story.

"I thought about my boys and my two girls and your mom. I wondered how you'd get along without me. I'd never see grandkids or go to Alaska. I shit myself, and this made him laugh even harder. I was really groveling then. He said he wouldn't kill me if I took a bite out of the guts of that elk. So I did. I had blood and elk shit all over my face. Then I threw up and this made him laugh like a madman. This stuff went on for what felt like forever. He was playing mind games with me. Torturing me. Finally, he made me cut off and stick the elk's privates in my mouth. He said he wished he had a camera, so he could take a picture to show my boys what a good cocksucker I was. And then right when I thought I was done for, he told me to go get in my truck and get out of here. I thanked him like I've never thanked anyone. I was just so grateful to be able to live another day. It was weird. It was almost as if not only was it his elk, but my life was also his to do with what he wanted. I would have helped him get the elk out, but he never thought of that, I guess. By the time I climbed that ridge and got to my truck, I was so tired, and so—oh I don't know—sad."

He took out another Pall Mall, and I could tell the story was taking its toll. He popped a nitro pill. *Dad, you can stop now. I get it,* I said in my head but not to him. I needed him to finish the story. I had to know. This was my only chance at getting my father back.

"My gun was still in the rack where I left it. It's strange, but I thought about using it on myself for a minute there. But then I was filled with a rage I didn't know I had. I think I must have screamed a bloodcurdling scream, and that guy—I think his name was Mike or something—heard it. I guess he realized that I killed that elk with something and maybe I might use it on him. He was right about that. I saw him making his way down the ridge with the elk head. He was about 250 yards or maybe farther. I had the crosshairs on his back and I fired a shot. I missed him. I wasn't too surprised because I was shaking like a leaf. Then he did a funny thing. He stopped by a tree and put the elk's head where his head should be. I guess he was tired of running, or forgot that a moving target is harder to hit than a stationary one. Well, I just fired one more shot at the head of that elk, and that son of a bitch went down. I watched for about ten or fifteen minutes and he didn't move, so I went down there to see. I saw the hole in his head—it was just above the left eye—and when I picked up that elk's head, it had a hole in it too. I guess that's why the bullet didn't go all the way through. I drug his body up near the elk's. There was a flat place in the ground just below the bull. I dug a little hole with a rock that I'd found and put him in it. That took a while. Then I rolled that elk over him, thinking no one would look for him there in a million years. Also, no one would think the buzzards were eating anything but rotten elk meat. I felt bad about that elk meat. I drove his truck three miles to the main road down in the bottom, and walked that three miles back up. I didn't want anyone to know he was in that area, just in case. I was lucky it was such a miserable rainy day. You know, I did not see one other car or truck besides his or mine."

"Did you really have to kill him?" I asked.

He looked at me and half smiled. "I didn't really weigh out the consequences or anything. I think I would have killed him even if the whole world was watching." He sighed deeply. "My only regret is that you know. If you want to turn me in, well, you do what you gotta do. You know the truth. What I did that day was right."

I just shook my head. I couldn't think about it. The news was too new. I couldn't get any perspective. Mark came walking down the road and Dad looked at me and shrugged. I shrugged back, not sure what either of us meant. Mark was oblivious about everything but the hunt. "Let's go get some meat, girls!" he yelled.

The rest of those ten days went by fast. We saw a lot of elk, and I actually got a shot off, but I missed. So that year we struck out during my hunt. Mark got a spike elk at the end of the season and a cooler of frozen elk showed up in Nashville a month or so later, a nice and unexpected surprise. Dad and I never spoke again about the murder of Michael J. Whiting, forty-five, of Junction City, Oregon.

The next year I took a day off from hunting and tracked down Michael J. Whiting, Jr., who was working in a Home Depot in Eugene. I told him I was working on a story about unsolved murder cases in the area. He had been eleven when his father turned up missing.

"So, what was your father like?" I asked innocently.

"I don't remember that much," he said, and then his voice began to crack, and I knew that wasn't true. "Oh, I promised my mother I'd respect her privacy, but honestly, mister, whoever killed my dad probably saved her." He wiped away a tear with the back of his hand. "Dad would have eventually killed her, or me. He was not a good person. I really don't want to go into it."

I assured him he didn't have to.

"If they ever find out who did it, I will personally thank them. You can print that."

After my "interview" with the son, I did indeed feel better. I don't know what that says about me. My dad did not kill in self-defense, and maybe the murder was premeditated. Maybe it was temporary insanity. I have to admit there is a part of me that lies awake and wonders if the apple doesn't fall far from the tree.

><

Tim Johnson

Tim Small Johnson grew up in a small logging community in western Oregon, and it's evident that his rural roots run deep in his words and his approach to music. His musical tastes and interests vary widely, but country music was—and always will be—his first love. Tim's early influences include artists such as Merle Haggard, Willie Nelson, Kris Kristofferson, and Waylon Jennings.

Tim's first cut was "The Struggling Years," recorded by the late, great Chris LeDoux. More than a decade later, Tim has scored over one hundred major label cuts, including such hits as "I Let Her Lie," "Thank God for Believers," "Things That Never Cross a Man's Mind" by Kellie Pickler, and Diamond Rio's moving single "God Only Cries." Tim's song "To Do What I Do" was recorded by Alan Jackson and inspired the title of his 2004 release What I Do. *Tim also wrote the song "When I Think About Leavin'" on Kenny Chesney's quadruple platinum album* When the Sun Goes Down.

Tim coproduced Blaine Larsen's first two albums, Off to Join the World *and* Rockin' You Tonight, *on Giantslayer/BNA Records.*

Will It Ever Happen Again?

★

Michael Kosser

Every week I make appointments to write songs with my friends. We get together at ASCAP or BMI or Joe's farm or my house over in Mt. Juliet. It's not always easy to do that. You see, my last hit came in 1992, and my last major album cut happened in 1994. Last week we celebrated my tenth consecutive year without a cut. Gallows humor is no humor—not when you take your life seriously.

I feel so sorry for my wife. We were married in 1982 and we struggled for years. Oh, we had dreams. I'd get big hits and she could stop working and we'd have a family and live like real people. I went seven years without making a dollar on my songs. Then when things happened, they happened suddenly. I wrote a couple of things with Duke Devery. Duke wrote for Hitlannd Music, and Hitlannd had a very hot plugger named Dwarf Duval.

One memorable week Dwarf got both of the songs I wrote with Duke recorded, one with Randy Travis and one with Alabama. For three months we waited, and sweated, and then within two weeks of each other, both Randy and Alabama had our songs out and on the radio. We watched the two records race each other up the charts. My wife and I went to the bank and borrowed money for a very nice little house. I began to listen to the radio every day, and most of the time I heard at least one of the songs.

Suddenly country music sounded so much better on the radio than it had when everyone *else* was getting all the hits. In October, when the BMI Awards came along, it seemed like that whole dinner was for *us*—me and Duke and my wife, and Dwarf, and the company owner, Mr. Crawford. They went up to the stage with us to collect the plaques, grinned at us, slapped us on the shoulders and called us "their boys."

That went on for three years—three years of cuts, and singles, and awards…and the checks, oh Lord the checks. My wife and I felt like such normal people that we started having kids—two of them, as I recall. Oh—and we'd be invited to sing our songs at the little writers' shows around town. Funny thing. Our songs weren't any better than when we weren't getting hits, but now that we had hits, we were considered expert songwriters. Folks *assumed* we knew what we were doing.

So did we? After three years of hits, did we have confidence? Oh yeah!

Maybe so. Duke and I would come into the Hitlannd building where they gave us our own little writer room and we'd get to work, and along about eleven, Dwarf would knock on the door and tell us we'd better get this one finished because Warner Bros. had put a hold on our last one for Travis Tritt. Then he'd take us to lunch. At lunch he'd sometimes talk about how he wished he could write like us, and how glad he was that he had the talent to pitch songs, and great songs to pitch like the ones we were writing. Oh man, did he gush. And we ate it up, along with the free food. All that money we were making, and we didn't even have to buy our own lunch. One time I called home to tell my mom that my song was being sung on the Leno show, and she called everyone in town about it. Later she sent me an article from the *Jamesville Sentinel* about us, me and Duke, and all the hits we were getting. Tell you what. I've saved all the Billboard charts that had our songs on them, saved all the articles I could find, even a couple of videos of our songs, taped right off TNN, but nothing satisfied quite so much as knowing that all the girls back in Jamesville who had turned their noses up at me would have to read about me. Hell, I could've written "How Do Ya Like Me Now" years before it was actually written—I wanted to. I did, in fact, more than once, but Dwarf just said it was too obnoxious. It'd never get cut. We never even saved a lyric.

I can remember sitting in the backyard at the house, watching the kids splashing in the wading pool, the sun a big red ball on the edge of the horizon, me looking at my wife as she watched the kids, a glow so warm around both of us, both of us believing this was gonna go on, and on, and on. *Living* like it was gonna go on and on and on. Disney World for the kids, new cars, a bigger house with a bigger yard. Don't tell me I didn't appreciate what we had. I appreciated every damn bit of it, and so did she—and that's why we wanted more of it.

Guess what? Me and Duke didn't split up to write with more famous writers. Dwarf didn't get drunk and run his car under an eighteen-wheeler. Hitlannd didn't sell out to Sony Tree. None of that happened. We didn't even stop getting cuts—not all at once. Just…just, one year the cuts (there were eleven of them) stopped turning into singles. And it happened that the albums they came out on were not multi-platinum. Soon our draws began to morph into debt. After about a year and a half of that, I began to notice that Dwarf would not bubble quite as much when he'd walk in, and when we'd play him our new song he'd say, "You better get a bastard demo on *that* one." Duke must have been hurt by stuff like that, because we weren't writing as often as we had. That's what happens to writing partners when the hits stop coming.

At the two-year mark without a hit, I noticed that Dwarf was beginning to say things like, "We need a hit, boys" a little too often to be a joke. Then came that third year, the first time in six years I didn't get a single song recorded on a major label. That was the year Mr. Crawford called me into his office and said, "Jack, been lookin' at your statements—you're into us pretty good, don't you think?"

I sighed. It wasn't unexpected, but it hurt. "Yeah, guess so." I wanted to ask him how about all the money we'd made him when we were making money—before they started pitching these three new guys they'd signed the year before. I wanted to tell him our new songs were the best in years. I wanted to beg him not to break up a winning team. And I wanted to tell him to shove a red-hot poker up his ungrateful butt.

Maybe, just maybe, the script should have called for him to say, "We're gonna pick up this last option, but this year better be a good year for you," because I knew this year *was* gonna be a good year for us, I just knew it. I *always* just knew it.

"Writers..." He sighed. "They have their time, then it's done."

What the hell did he mean, "done"? "Have you heard our new stuff?" I asked. Stupid question. Mr. Crawford was not a music man. Mr. Crawford listened to Dwarf. It was Dwarf who had told him to cut us loose.

Only it wasn't us they'd cut loose, it was just me. Duke had seen the writing on the wall before I had, and after hours he'd started writing with our song plugger. Dwarf was a salesman.

He could get the job done when he really wanted to. I didn't know it, but Duke and Dwarf had four songs on hold the day Mr. Crawford cut me loose.

So there I was, without a deal after six years. I tried to find new writing partners, but I was about two years too cold for any of the good ones to be interested. I went to all the publishers who had tried to woo me away from Hitlannd in the good old days, and not a one of them had the guts to turn me down right then. They all said they liked my songs and they'd see if they had the money to do a deal and they'd get back to me.

I guess I got discouraged pretty quickly. I went to everybody I knew on Music Row who had a job and liked me. I asked for advice and got sympathy but nothing else. One person who grew short on sympathy after about nine months of that was my wife. I'm not gonna be too hard on her. She had worked at Kroger for eight years without complaint, waiting for me to turn a trick or two for us. She'd beamed with pride at every success. She'd found her dream: raising a family and taking care of a happy, fulfilled husband. We had passed through that moment of concern when it seemed every young female songwriter had me in their sights and we had emerged without a scratch.

Now, suddenly, it seemed like we were back to square one. Money was running out, the mortgage was too high, our car payments were high, the kids were expensive items, bless their little hearts. We'd have to downsize—not the kids, everything else. Such a nice simple word, downsize—means selling this, buying that, losing this, keeping that, meanwhile knowing that when it was all done we would be coated with a rancid layer of failure. And she would have to go back to Kroger.

Oh, no she wouldn't. That's what she told me the night we moved into a precious little cottage we'd found in South

Nashville, a place stuck in a pocket that the developers had forgotten, with a grassy yard, trees, surrounded by country folks living in the city, a long way from the West Meade climb we had made, only to fall. "I am not going to put these kids in day care," she said, her teeth clenched in barely suppressed fury. "They are going to have a mo-ther!"

I knew what that meant. I was going to have to get a job—not a music-business job, a *job* job. My wife was telling me that I had, after all, failed to achieve a career as a professional songwriter. I could not accept that.

"We still have some money in the bank," I said. "I'll find a deal. I'll have a hit. I'll make it back! I was ranting. I knew I was, but I was not going to admit to being a loser, not after all those wonderful, glamorous victories.

"This is a stupid business," she snarled. "And we are stupid for believing in it. I am not going to see us lose the money we have left, then sell the house, move back into a tiny apartment with two growing kids. And I am not going to watch you lose your mind because we've lost everything else. Let's go on to something else while we still have something left!"

I knew she was right, of course, but I wasn't ready. Eyes filled with indignant tears, I stormed out of the house, stopped at the first Krystal and gobbled down six Krystal burgers, then headed out to the Old Red Lounge. It was always Writers' Night down at the Old Red Lounge.

I suppose a part of me expected to run into Roberta, or somebody like Roberta. I don't think she would have given me a second look if my friend Lex hadn't introduced me to her. "He wrote..." and began the roll call of hits while I stared at her modestly. She nodded and studied me as if deciding whether my track record made up for my buffless body. She chose career over romance, allowed me to lead her to the table, and made a serious attempt at being attracted to me. I told her my wife didn't understand and she understood. I told her I wanted to hear her songs and she did not have to feign enthusiasm. I had had hits. I must be connected. I was worth her time. That was good enough for her and good enough for me.

It was her turn to get up onstage and sing. Her songs were not awful. In fact they were quite good. They didn't have a prayer of being recorded, but, you know, they were good songs. And I told her so.

"You really mean it?" she asked.

"I said it. That means I mean it." I sounded very sincere.

Now it was her turn. "I didn't know who wrote those songs," she said. "They've always been among my favorites. You're really nice. I'm sorry your wife doesn't understand you. You have gorgeous eyes. Do you have a place to stay tonight?"

She was working very fast, and her timing was just right. This girl obviously knew quality when she saw it. Tonight she was a ten. My wife was a one. End of story.

There weren't enough writers that night and she went up for an encore. While she was singing her song I was writing my own, about a guy who was such an idiot that he gave up everything he had won over the past six years. I pictured coming home and telling my wife I was leaving her for a young girl who understands. Pictured her tears. Pictured the kids' tears. Pictured waking up next to my new torrid love the next morning. Were divorce songs selling these days? I hated the song and went no further with it. In fact, in the middle of her last chorus, I waved to her, smiled, blew her a kiss, gave her a thumbs-up, and headed out the door.

I drove home and walked in the house, not guilty but gruff. "I'm *not* looking for work!" I growled. Her eyebrows raised. She knew more was coming.

"Not tomorrow. You got any ideas?"

"You could start by substitute teaching," she said. "That'd get a little money coming in. I can work at Kroger on the weekends if you'll take care of the kids. *I'm* not giving up on your dream," she said. "I just hope you consider that there are *other* dreams." She smiled. "And we did get to live your dream—for a while. Most dreams are just like that. They last a little while. Then you wake up."

It was my turn to smile. I was wide awake, and I liked it fine.

❧

Michael Kosser

Michael Kosser is a senior editor at American Songwriter *magazine, where he has written a column on songwriting called "Street Smarts" for the past twenty years. He has also written seventeen published books, including, most recently, the award-winning* How Nashville Became Music City, USA. *His songs have been recorded by George Jones, Conway Twitty, Tammy Wynette, Barbara Mandrell, Charlie Rich, Ray Price, Marty Robbins, the Kendalls, Blake Shelton, Josh Gracin, and many more.*

With Gratitude

First and foremost, the editors would like to thank the songwriters who ventured out into sometimes uncharted territories—writing something without music and longer than four minutes in length. This collection is the fruit of their labor and their passion. We would be remiss if we didn't thank all their families, management, and staff who nudged them forward when we couldn't.

Our agent, Jeff Kleinman of Folio Literary Agency, ventured into a world he knew little about when he took on a collection of short stories by songwriters. Yet, with his signature passion coupled with wisdom and common sense, he became our advocate to find the perfect home for this collection. We are forever indebted to Jeff.

Then there is Rolf Zettersten, our esteemed publisher at Center Street, who was willing to buy into our belief that songwriters were, as Vince Gill called them, "the ultimate short, short story writers." We are forever aware that without your faith, no one would be reading this now.

We want to thank Chris Park, briefly our editor, who

convinced the folks at Hachette that we were not crazy. We are forever indebted to her for leaving us in the capable hands of Christina Boys, our amazing ace editor whose hard work and superior intellect makes us all appear much smarter than we are. Like Rolf, she "got it" and has run with it ever since. Then there is Meredith Pharaoh, our assistant editor, for helping with the seemingly never-ending work load we dumped upon her and all the rest of the Center Street/Hachette gang: Lori Quinn, who has added her passion for a job well done to the mix along with Harry Helm, Jana Burson, Preston Cannon, Jody Waldrup, and Dylan Hoke. Not to mention anyone and everyone else we really should be thanking, but haven't. Thank you.

Thanks to Amy Grant and Vince Gill, Tamara Saviano, Jay Jones, Ellen Pryor, Robert Clement, and Doug Waterman of *American Songwriter* magazine, John Carter Cash, John Allen, Koz Weaver, Bob Sullivan, Doug Howard, Terry Moran, Bart Herbison, Judi Marshall, Angie Gore, and Paula Szeigis.

John would especially like to acknowledge:

August Christopher Bohlinger, the most inspired and inspiring person I have ever known. To Aug's mamma, for giving me this beautiful son. To Megan Mullins, my proofreader, cowriter, muse, and much more. To my parents, John and Bette Bohlinger, who are the salt of the earth, living out their lives to make this world a better place for those in need. My partners, Robert Hicks and Justin Stelter, who took a simple idea, developed it into so much more, and tenaciously ran with it for over five years.

Unending gratitude to my loyal friends at *Nashville Star*, particularly Ben Silverman, Howard T. Owens, Jon Small, Jeff Boggs, and Don Lepore; my sibs/support group: Jeanne

Cox, Jan Osborne, JoLynn Sommers, Mark Bohlinger, and Nick Bohlinger; Dave Goodwin, my brother and partner in "A MAJOR CONGLOMERATE"; 262five's Kyle Gustie and Brinson Strickland; Eddie Tidwell: great friend and music encyclopedia; the Mullins family; Donnie Fritts; Larry Boothby; Michael Spriggs; Tracy Gershon; Katherine Lepore, Billy Block, Bob Kirsh, Jonah Rabinowitz, and Lynn Adelman of the W. O. Smith School; Randy Owen; Ray Scott; Trent Summar; Shawn Pennington; Tracy Gershon; Arthur Buenahora; Clay Bradley; Loretta Fellin; Ashley Ray; Judy Bell; Brooke Lee; Stan Moress; the Richmond Organization; and all of the musicians and artists who, for nearly a decade, have employed me, thus keeping me safe from engaging in any activity that even vaguely resembles work.

Justin would especially like to acknowledge:

First and foremost, Robert Hicks and John Bohlinger for including me. Without them I would never have been a part of this amazing project. However, most importantly, I'd like to thank Olivia Stelter, my lovely wife, for her compassion and patience through all these years. I'd like to thank Keith Stelter, my grandfather, and Imogene Bolin and Tom Neff for setting the standard of pursuing life with passion; Kevin Stelter, my father, for constantly inspiring me to be a better person; Mark Stelter, my uncle, for unending encouragement; Dena and Tim Wilson and Sherry and Bill Bolin for reminding me to have faith; my two sisters, Shae and Skye Stelter; and all other family members, including Great-Grandma Naomi Draggoo, Kay Stelter, Gracia and Dennis Draggoo, Audrey and Bill Fields (who first introduced me to Western literature when I was twelve), Horace (one of the bravest men I know), his wife, Willa Dean Dunn, and Jodi Stelter.

Tom Strawman has been a source of steady guidance since my first writing course in college. To Travis Billings and Danny Cunningham, two of the best friends anyone could have. To Robert Hicks, Adam Goodheart, Duncan Murrell and Jill Robinson, all great writers I'm fortunate enough to call my friends.

Then there are Catherine Anderson, Danny Anderson, Angela and Porter Calhoun, Duke Ellis, Diana and Gary Fisketjon, Mary and Winder Heller (the happiest people I know), Kay and Rod Heller, Lark Foster, Kathy and Justin Neibank, Annie Owen, Mimi and Sokrates Pantelides, Ann and Aaron Reed, Beth and Peter Thevenot (tied for the happiest people I know), and Rick Warwick.

Robert would especially like to acknowledge:

My parents, who gave me a passion for words, for stories, for music. Anything I've done in this life, of any real value, begins with them. Likewise, my brother, Marcus, his wife, Candy, my niece, Nova, and Danny, her husband, continue to remind me about how far passion, kindness, and curiosity really can take you in this world.

I'd like to thank John Bohlinger for sharing his idea for this collection with me. I'd like to thank Justin Stelter for his hard work and persistence to see it to completion. I want to thank both of them for letting me be a part of this partnership.

I would like to thank my dear friend, Hazel Smith, who has spent years reminding me that Country Music is like Our Lord in that it must be in our hearts to be real.

My coeditors have already covered many of those who I would be thanking here. I can only hope that those already listed know how much they mean to me. A few more of the support team of friends that have cheered me on over the years, not mentioned above, are Julian Bibb, Kelly and Bo Bills, Joe Cashia, Mary-Springs and Stephane Couteaud, George Ducas, Jim Duff, Amy Einhorn, Becki Foster, Matt Futterman, Andrew Glasgow, Monte Isom, Curt Jones, Evan Lowenstein, Riley May, Martha Otis, Tommy Peters, Jamie Raab, Charlie Snow, and Karen Torres. Finally, there is that very long list of bookstore folks who may be the best demographic of men and women I have ever had the privilege to know. Your encouragement and friendship are not long forgotten.

An Interview with
the Editors

*Robert Hicks, John Bohlinger,
and Justin Stelter*

1. How did you decide to put together this collection?

JB: I grew up writing songs, making them up before I could write. I pounded them out on my family's tragically out of tune upright whose sticky keys hit me right at eye level. I smacked my dad's Tijuana gut-string, holding it like a doghouse bass and hollering out impromptu lyrics about my dog, cat, shoes, brother—a childhood stream of semi-consciousness in rhyme. Haunted by these melodies and lyrics that woke me up at night, I'd forget where I was going, where I parked my car, what I was supposed to be doing. So I set out on a quixotic journey to Nashville to be a songwriter. I waited tables at night, wrote songs on bar napkins that morphed into hard paper balls in my pockets, woke up early and wrote all day as my son and I played pirates or cowboys in the strip of grass outside our little crappy apartment. I pitched songs all over town to every publisher, artist, plugger, record executive, or poser I met. Eventually I parlayed hard work and average talent into a good little career. (What a delicious scam.) The driving force behind my preoccupation remains the power of a song. Today, just like when I was a kid listening to the radio in our '72 Microbus, a great song hypnotizes me, taking the entire roller coaster ride of emotions that you feel in a week and squeezing it into a few compact minutes where time stops.

In Nashville, songwriters strive to find that magic marriage of lyrics and melody that says the ineffable. Sometimes the lyrics alone, like the melody alone, can give you that feeling. I started hunting for short stories by Nashville writers, devoured what I found, and began writing my own stories. I talked to my songwriter and publisher friends and found many of them were writing prose as well or collecting short stories by songwriters. I contacted my longtime friend Robert Hicks. Robert and I met through songwriting and share the same passion for the craft. We joined forces to record short stories by Nashville songwriters, like John Lomax chasing the blues of the Delta to share with the world. Robert brought in Justin. We plugged away for six years, searching for songs and a home for the project, and lucked out with Center Street.

2. How did you come to know the contributors?

RH: In 1969 I came to Nashville to go to college. All I knew about country music was that I didn't like it.

But somehow, through proximity, or happenstance, one night I stumbled into the briar patch of country music: the alley next to the historic Ryman Auditorium—"the Mother Church of Country Music"—which, back then, still housed the Grand Ole Opry. In those days, the alley served as a de facto back stage of the Ryman, which had been built as a church and hence didn't have a back stage.

That night, a bunch of folks lounged against the walls of the alley, smoking cigarettes and laughing. A beautiful woman, overdressed, began to argue with a man. As their fight grew louder, it seemed to amuse everyone else. They were married, I realized. The argument escalated with accusations of infidelity; she shoved him, and he pushed back; and just as it all seemed to be transforming into a bizarre scene from a Robert Altman movie, a kid came bounding down the side steps of the Ryman and yelled, "You're on in five minutes, Ms. Anderson!"

The woman stopped, turned to her husband, said, "Help me with my makeup." And just about five minutes later, Lynn Anderson stood on the stage of the Opry singing "I Never Promised You a Rose Garden."

Somehow, at that moment, I fell in love with country music. These folks wore their feelings like they wore their rhinestones. Everything shone, and nothing was hidden. It seemed like a good way to live.

A few years later, after finishing school and still a bit directionless, I sat in a bar with an old friend. Our discussion was part of that unending discussion you have at that age about what to do with your life. For whatever reason, he turned and said, "I think you should be a music publisher."

"Really?" I asked. "What do they do?"

"I don't know, but I think you'd be good at it—it's a good title."

I was looking for answers, and thankfully he wasn't in a cult or I guess I might be chanting in an airport somewhere today. Instead, the next day I ended up at a bookstore, reading about music publishing—and I decided that this was what I wanted to do with my life: be an advocate of and believer in the songwriter. These were people I wanted to cast in my lot with. It's now my world and a world I believe in very deeply.

Nashville is a small town in many ways; even more important, it's one of the most accessible places on earth for the creative. Many of the contributors in this book are not only colleagues but also life-long friends.

3. Was there a particular story that you related to?

JS: There were so many stories I related to. But maybe Tim Putnam's "The River" is as near and dear to me as anything in the book. I grew up on Westerns. My passion for reading is born out of them. They took me beyond the world of my childhood and taught me about honor and justice and manliness. My reading taste has expanded a bit over the years, but I still have a heart for those stories. When Robert and I joined forces with John, I had no thought that a Western would ever show up. Yet, there it was one day. Somehow it had all come full circle for me.

JB: Louis Armstrong said, "If they act too hip, you know they can't play." Nashville songwriters carry that same philosophy about writers. The emperor's clothes bit may work in pop where listeners fear that if they don't understand they must be stupid or square, but not in Nashville. Country music is the poetry of the guy who changes oil at Wal-Mart all day, or the girl behind the cashier's register, worried about raising her kid alone. Nashville writers say what we have felt. Like Harlan said, "Three chords and the truth." Tom T. epitomizes the best of these Nashville writers. His story, "The Day Jimmy Killed the Rabbit," pulls you in like his songs do and sucker punches you in the gut at the end, leaving you gasping for air and wishing you could have fixed this kid's problems because that could have been you—or your cousin, spouse, mom, son, somebody you love.

4. What story most surprised you?

JS: Every single story in the collection confirms our theory that these men and women—and all the rest of the songwriters in Nashville—really are some of the best storytellers there are. Yet, that said, I have to admit that there was always a bit of genuine surprise every time I finished reading a story, since another songwriter had just proved us right again. As far as a surprise within the story itself: Well, I hate to admit it, for I should have seen it coming from the beginning, but I guess that would be the end of Bobby Braddock's story.

5. Which story particularly reflected the person who wrote it? Which did not?

RH: This is a tough question for me to answer—not because I don't know which stories reflect the people who wrote them, but because so many of the folks are friends, and I know how close to home they were treading.

You know, on second thought, I think I will plead the Fifth and move on.

6. Robert and John, how did you come up with the ideas for your own stories?

JB: During my earlier years in Nashville, a series of bad breaks left my son, his mamma, and me living in our van for a week. It tore me up to think my stupidity had put them in such a mess. My sweet son had no idea we were poor; he thought we were camping. Getting through that opened my eyes, gave me empathy for our brothers and sisters who struggle with poverty. I saw first hand the emptiness of some charity that benefits the giver rather than the receiver. "A Big Batch of Biscuits" isn't fiction, it's a retelling of the experience a friend of mine went through.

RH: I have never claimed to have an original idea in my life. My ideas come from the world I live in and know well. The story in this book—like all the rest of the stories I recount—originates in reality. It should not come as much of a surprise to those who know me when I say I come from a crazy family. In the story I've provided here, most of the narrative is way more true than I'd like to admit—although I did change a few details here and there, without altering, I hope, the essential truths behind it. Now most of that part of my family is gone, so it's a little easier to tell their tales; but still, telling their story is mixed with bittersweet guilt. Again, perhaps I should plead the Fifth on this one too...